A Nation Collapses

A *Nation Collapses* revises the traditional understanding of a critical moment in the history of World War II: the collapse of the Italian Fascist regime and Italy's unconditional surrender in September 1943. Drawing on massive, mostly unpublished documents, the book analyzes the course of the secret negotiations between Italy and Britain before the overthrow of Mussolini in July 1943 and finds that both parties negotiated in bad faith and with a great deal of duplicity. Misjudging their Axis partner, Nazi Germany, as well as the Allied powers, the Italians both overestimated the extent of the Allies' strategic commitment in Italy and promised their conquerors a degree of military assistance they were in no condition to deliver. The Italian army, bereft of leadership or guidance, swiftly fell into disarray, and hundreds of thousands of troops were rounded up by the Germans and interned in concentration camps. As the Anglo-American troops that controlled southern Italy advanced into the German-occupied north, the country, ravaged by a mounting civil war, became a battlefield for the opposing armies for twenty long months.

Elena Agarossi is Professor of Contemporary History at the University of Aquila and at Scuola Superiore della Pubblica Amministrazione in Rome (Institute for Advanced Studies in Public Administration). She has taught at the Universities of Padua, Pisa, Palermo, and Rome. She has held fellowships at the Woodrow Wilson International Center, Oxford University, British Academy of Sciences, Center for European Studies, Harvard University and Center for European Studies, and Stanford University. Among her publications are *Operation Sunrise* (with B. Smith), New York: Basic Books, 1979 (also published in Italian, German, and Chinese); *Gli Stati Uniti e le origini della guerra fredda*, Bologna: Mulino, 1984; *L'Italia nella sconfitta*, Naples: ESI, 1985; *L'inganno reciproco*, Rome: Ministero dei Beni Culturali, 1993; and *Togliatti e Stalin* (with V. Zaslavsky), Bologna: Mulino, 1997, recipient of the Acqui Storia Prize for 1998. The Italian edition of the present book, *Una nazione allo sbando*, Bologna: Mulino, 1993, received the 1995 Walter Tobagi Prize for history books.

A Nation Collapses

THE ITALIAN SURRENDER OF SEPTEMBER 1943

Elena Agarossi

Translated by Harvey Fergusson II

CAMBRIDGE
UNIVERSITY PRESS

PUBLISHED BY THE PRESS SYNDICATE OF THE UNIVERSITY OF CAMBRIDGE
The Pitt Building, Trumpington Street, Cambridge, United Kingdom

CAMBRIDGE UNIVERSITY PRESS
The Edinburgh Building, Cambridge CB2 2RU, UK   http: www.cup.cam.ac.uk
40 West 20th Street, New York, NY 10011-4211, USA   http: www.cup.org
10 Stamford Road, Oakleigh, Melbourne 3166, Australia
Ruiz de Alarcón 13, 28014 Madrid, Spain

First published 2000

Printed in the United States of America

Typeface Sabon 10.25/14 pt.   *System* QuarkXPress [BTS]

A catalog record for this book is available from the British Library.

Library of Congress Cataloging-in-Publication Data
Aga Rossi, Elena.
A nation collapses: the Italian surrender of September 1943 /
Elena Agarossi.
[Una nazione allosbando]
p. cm.
Includes index.
ISBN 0-521-59199-6
1. World War, 1939–1945 – Italy.   2. Italy – History – Allied
occupation, 1943–1947. I. Title.
D763.I8A537   1999
940.53'45 – dc21   98-45622
                                                          CIP

ISBN 0 521 59199 6 hardback

Contents

Note on Archival Sources

The reconstruction of circumstances, events and political choices that resulted in the Italian acceptance of unconditional surrender and exit from the alliance with Nazi Germany had to be based mainly on archival sources, because secondary sources are insufficient and, in the case of the Italian ones, often unreliable. This study has required a comparative analysis of the documents preserved in the American, British and Italian archives. The Italian documentation presents a special problem because many of the original records on the armistice negotiations were burned on September 9, 1943, when armistice was announced. The existing documents may well include false ones, created subsequently when some of the Italian generals were called upon to justify their actions before a military tribunal. In spite of this problem, the documents housed in the Archive of the Historical Office of the Army General Staff – AUSSME in Italian – constitute the most important collection of records used in the preparation of this book. Until a few years ago this study could not have been written, since the AUSSME archive was closed to scholars, as was the Historical Archive of the Navy (ASM), which contains the important memoir of Admiral Raffaele de Courten, the Italian minister of the navy, and other documents that are crucial for the historical reconstruction of the fleet's actions after September 8, 1943.

Both the Italian commanders' accounts of events following the announcement of the armistice and the testimonies gathered by the Commission of Inquiry chaired by Mario Palermo between 1944 and 1945 are very useful. However, they must be used with caution because there are differences among them, even on fundamental points, and in many cases they are tainted by obvious self-serving intentions. The veracity of the Italian documentation can be assessed, however, by comparing it with the existing Anglo-American records of the negotiations carried out in Lisbon and in the small Sicilian village of Cassibile and of the telegrams exchanged between the Italian Supreme Command and the Allied Force Headquarters in Algiers from September 1 to September 9, 1943.

A further limitation of the Italian records is the nearly total absence of documentation on the position of the Italian government. The available Italian documents, in fact, come mostly from the Historical Office of the Army General Staff and the Historical Archive of the Navy, since little or nothing of importance on the armistice has been preserved in the Ministry of Foreign Affairs or in the central government archives.

The documentation in the British and American archives is much richer, but inexplicably it has never been used by Italian scholars, even if it has remained for the most part accessible to the public. Following the messages exchanged in 1943 between Washington, London, Algiers and Rome, historians can now identify the positions taken by both the chief military leaders, such as General Eisenhower, and the political ones, mainly Roosevelt, Churchill and Eden, and analyze the Allied decision-making process. The British documents come from the Public Record Office, the American ones from several archives, with the largest collections being preserved in the National Archives in Washington, D.C., the Franklin Delano Roosevelt Library in Hyde Park, New York, and the Eisenhower Library, in Abilene, Kansas.

Among the British documents, the file entitled *The Italian Armistice*, based largely on unpublished documents from the Public Record Office, occupies a special place. Compiled by Patricia McCallum as preparatory work for the British official history of World War II by Michael Howard, *The Italian Armistice* is still the most exhaustive contribution to the history of British policy toward Italy in the period 1940–43.

Note on Archival Sources

Other important collections of military documents are those of the British–American Combined Chiefs of Staff (CSS) and of the Allied Force Headquarters for the Mediterranean theater (AFHQ), which have been divided between the Public Record Office, London, and the National Archives in Washington. The collection *Capitulation of Italy*, in the papers of General Walter Bedell Smith in the Eisenhower Library, is of special value, since it contains almost the entire series of messages exchanged between Rome and Algiers on the eve of the armistice proclamation.

For the Allied decision-making process regarding the military strategy for the Mediterranean and the policy toward Italy, Roosevelt's papers – especially the files MR 34/Italy; MR 166, Naval Aide's File (Surrender of Italy); and Churchill's papers (especially PREM 3) – are indispensable. While the State Department was not involved in the decisions, the Foreign Office played a large role; thus its papers at the Public Record Office (FO371) and the papers of Lord Avon (Anthony Eden) are valuable. Reflecting the marginal role of the American and British secret services in the organization of the Italian armistice, little useful information can be found in the papers of the Office of Strategic Services (OSS) or in the Special Operation Executive (SOE), whose files for Italy were opened to scholars at the PRO in July 1998. Other useful collections for this book include the General Harold Alexander Papers and the War Office Papers (WO204) in the PRO, the War Department Papers (ASW) in the National Archives, the Stimson Papers at Yale University and the Robert Murphy Papers at Hoover Library, Stanford University, California.

Abbreviations

AFHQ	Allied Force Headquarters
ASM	Archivio Storico della Marina
ASW	Office of the Assistant Secretary of War
AUSSME	Archivio dell'Ufficio Storico dello Stato maggiore dell'Esercito
CAB	Cabinet Papers, Public Record Office, London
CCS	Combined Chiefs of Staff, United States and Great Britain
DDI	Ministero degli Affari esteri, *I documenti diplomatici italiani*
FDRL	Franklin Delano Roosevelt Library, Hyde Park, New York
FO	Foreign Office, Great Britain
FRUS	Department of State, *Foreign Relations of the United States*, Washington, D.C.
MEDTO	Mediterranean Theater of Operations
NA	National Archives, Washington, D.C.
OSS	Office of Strategic Services
OWI	Office of War Information
PREM 3	Premier; Public Record Office, London
PRO	Public Record Office, London
RG	Record Group
SIM	Servizio Informazioni Militari, Italy
SOE	Special Operation Executive, Great Britain
WO	War Office

Introduction

The armistice between Italy and the Allies on September 8, 1943, marked a decisive turning point in World War II, both on an international level and regarding Italy's internal affairs. The armistice signaled the imminent fall of the Axis and the final victory of the Allies. It also demonstrated the ineptitude of the Italian political and military elite, as well as the inability of the monarchy to lead the country out of the war and sever its Fascist connections, an inability that sealed the monarchy's fate.

September 8, 1943, has come to be regarded by Italians as one of the most tragic moments in the history of united Italy. It has become a symbol not only of the total collapse and dissolution of the state, but also of a deeply rooted crisis of the nation itself. The announcement of the armistice was followed by the precipitous flight from Rome of King Victor Emmanuel III, the government of Marshal Pietro Badoglio and the Supreme Command of the armed forces. The highest authorities of the land left as their only directive to the Italian armed forces the last words of the proclamation read on the radio by Prime Minister Badoglio as he announced the armistice: they were to cease hostilities against the Anglo-American forces, but retaliate "against any attack from any direction whatsoever."

The consequences of these events were devastating for Italy. An army of more than a million men disintegrated almost completely within a few days. Some units chose to go on fighting the Germans, and in some cases they held out for several weeks, but the results

1

were tragic. Since Italy had not yet declared war on Germany, Italian soldiers who offered armed resistance were considered *francs-tireurs* and many were shot, on Hitler's express orders. Now that the short-lived and illusory plan to withdraw from the conflict and immediately join the Anglo-Americans, thus avoiding the disgrace of being a defeated enemy, was no longer viable, Italy was abandoned to the violent revenge of the Germans, who savagely repressed any attempt by the Italian army to react, and deported and interned in Germany 700,000 Italian military personnel. The Nazi occupation of a large part of Italy, which became an enormous battlefield between the two opposing armies, was accompanied by increasingly violent repression of the civilian population and of the resistance movement that had developed in the country.

The course of events and the series of political decisions that brought the two sides to the conclusion of the armistice and its political and military consequences are worthy of study in all their complexity. However, although the tragedy of the September 8 armistice is frequently cited, it rarely has been analyzed in depth.[1]

There are still several questions that need final answers. What commitments were made by both sides at the time the armistice was signed? What goals were set by the governments involved, and which of these were met? How can one explain the total lack of direction among the Italian political and military leaders at this crucial moment in Italian history? What policy were the Allies following? What were the results of the imposition of unconditional surrender on Italy? What was Germany's strategy? Was the disaster of September 8 inevitable? What exactly happened to the Italian armed forces starting on September 8? Would it have been possible for Italy to change sides and collaborate effectively with the Anglo-Americans? And if so, why did it not do so?

Historians are still providing contradictory answers to these questions. Many aspects of the events that led the king and Badoglio to their decision to abandon the war and the complex negotiations that ended with the signing of the two armistice documents between Italy and the Allied governments have still not been fully clarified in historical writing, and they have been interpreted in different ways. For many years the commitments made by the two sides, amid mutual mistrust aggravated by disinformation and erroneous judgments of the actual military situation, as well as by the conduct of the Badoglio government, have continued to be the subject of controversies and disputed interpretations. The obvious interconnection of the events leading to the armistice, the failure to defend Rome, the disintegration of the Italian army and the German occupation have raised the issues of to what extent the government and the monarchy were responsible, and what alternatives were available at the time.

The need to shed light on these events induced the first anti-Fascist government, under Ivanoe Bonomi, to open an investigation as early as the fall of 1944, although the Anglo-Americans obliged Bonomi to limit his inquiry to the failure to defend Rome, in order to prevent the signatories of the armistice from being put on trial.[2] The Commission of Inquiry was chaired by Mario Palermo, a civilian attorney, and its members included Generals Pietro Ago and Luigi Amantea. In the face of many difficulties, the Palermo Commission exposed the grave responsibilities of the Badoglio government, the king and the Supreme Command for the collapse of the armed forces and the surrender of Rome to the Germans. The Commission's work was crucial because of the mass of material it assembled, but it could not lead to a formal indictment. In concluding his work, Palermo had to limit himself to requesting an expansion of the inquiry "for the purpose of ascertaining the extent to which both the military and the political leadership were to blame."[3]

At the time the Palermo Commission was performing its tasks, the High Commission for Sanctions against Fascism, established by a law of July 1944, had also opened its proceedings. The communist Mauro Scoccimarro, deputy chairman of the High Commission, instituted proceedings to purge many high-ranking officials from the public administration. Several generals were discharged for their failure to defend Rome. Generals Pentimalli and Del Tetto were arrested for their failure to defend Naples, and an attempt was made to indict Badoglio himself.[4] However, Scoccimarro's move was blocked by the reaction within the Bonomi government provoking the resignation of two ministers (Marcello Soleri of the treasury and Admiral Raffaele de Courten of the navy) and then of Bonomi himself. The replacement of Scoccimarro in the High Commission was a clear signal that the purge had run its course.

A third inquiry into the "behavior of officers at and following the announcement of the armistice" began in December 1943. It was initiated on Badoglio's behalf by the chief of the general staff, General Giovanni Messe, just nominated to replace Vittorio Ambrosio, who had been removed because of his Fascist past. However, given Badoglio's personal responsibility and the reticence of the upper reaches of the military, the largely negative findings of this inquest are not surprising. They indicate, although with some exceptions, an intention to conceal the truth rather than to shed light on it.[5]

Both the Palermo Commission and the Supreme Command's inquiry produced an enormous mass of material, which is fundamental for narrating the events of those days. It also serves to demonstrate that those who were most responsible systematically attempted to falsify the facts through their contradictory testimony, to excuse themselves from all culpability through reticent omissions and to support the assertion that the September 8 armistice announcement caught the government and the military commands completely by surprise. In the thousands of pages describing these events, from the first discussions of measures to be taken, to the flight of the highest officials of the state and the disintegration of the army – which was left without orders and at the mercy of the Germans – none of the principal officials admitted even partial responsibility for this national catastrophe. In 1947 the failure to defend Rome was reexamined for the last time by a military tribunal, which limited itself to investigating the operations of Generals Giacomo Carboni, in charge of Rome's defense, and Mario Roatta, chief of staff of the army, concluding two years later with a verdict of not guilty. In conclusion, the tribunal's verdict did not end the manipulation of facts, nor did it shed light on the falsehoods that helped to obfuscate the entire matter.[6]

Introduction

Memoirs discussing the armistice negotiations were for the most part deliberately distorted, and must therefore be consulted with great caution.[7] Nearly all the protagonists published their version of the events of the period, often to exculpate themselves, more often blaming others than bringing out the truth. Another reason for the difficulty of painting a convincing historical picture lies in the lack of Italian documents, which is only partially attributable to the need for secrecy during both the initial investigations and the negotiations. The Italians destroyed many documents that might have fallen into German or Anglo-American hands or were considered compromising; the Germans seized others; and many have disappeared.[8] The existing documents are preserved for the most part at the Historical Office of the Italian Army General Staff, but for a long time the Office was not open for consultation, so that it saw no need for an inventory. Only in the past few years has it been made accessible to scholars.

These are perhaps the objective reasons why Italian historical writing concerning September 8, 1943, has told only part of the story. There is still no scholarly sound, complete exposition. In the wake of the protagonists' memoirs published immediately after the war, whose limitations have already been mentioned, the writing of history has continued to be ex parte. Some authors blamed the king and the Badoglio government for the disintegration of the army; others, in order to justify the conduct of the monarchy, exaggerated the number of German units in Italy and claimed that the Anglo-Americans had deceived the Italians by anticipating the announcement of the armistice.[9]

Evaluating and interpreting the relations between the Italian authorities and the Anglo-Americans before the armistice are prerequisites to a historical judgment of the Italian government's actions at the moment of the surrender. The importance of British and American studies and archival documentation for an objective account of these events must be stressed.[10] The British and American memoirs are especially rich. After the volumes published immediately following the war, another cycle began in the 1960s when the memoirs of some of the most important Allied protagonists were published: those of Robert Murphy, Harold Macmillan, Kenneth Strong and Harold Nicolson. These were followed in the 1970s and 1980s by the diaries of Alexander Cadogan, Harold Macmillan and Robert Lockhart.[11]

This rich and more or less recent historical writing has not been used much in Italy, and the vast documentation in the British and American archives is not well known. In the absence of a thorough comparison with the Anglo-American sources, some versions of events from protagonists interested in defending their actions have been commonly accepted. Biased interpretations and even falsifications asserted from the very beginning have so deeply penetrated the collective consciousness as to become commonplace and sometimes uncritically accepted in Italian historical writing.[12]

To overcome such widespread disinformation, a historical analysis of the Italian armistice cannot be undertaken without considering the international context or without comparing the Italian and more reliable Anglo-American sources, even more so now that it is possible to reconstruct fully the decision-making processes among the Allies and the development of the various positions taken.

We still do not know enough about the military events of September 8 and of the following days, aside from what has been written in a few books and articles about isolated episodes. There is as yet no systematic study of the Italian armed forces that gives an account of the remote and contingent causes of their collapse, of the individual and collective acts of valor in opposing the Germans or of the ferocious German reprisals. The histories of World War II published in Italy rarely mention the events involving Italian soldiers after September 8. The armed defense of Rome and the resistance of the Acqui Division on the island of Cephalonia, which concluded with the shooting of more than five thousand Italian officers and soldiers by the Germans, have attracted much attention in recent years. They are certainly among the most emblematic examples of resistance in Italy and the Balkans, but there were many others that historians have ignored.[13] The instances of single detachments refusing to surrender were more numerous than acknowledged until recently. The deeply rooted image in both historical accounts and in public opinion of the armistice has led to a condemnation of the whole Italian military class. This negative view has resulted in an underestimation of the role played by Italian officers and other military personnel in the creation of the first bands of partisans and their active presence in the Resistance, as well as their participation in the liberation of Italy as members of the combat groups within the Allied armies.

In the past few years a number of fresh contributions have been made to the history of both the armed resistance by the Italian military and the "passive" one, in the form of soldiers' refusal, while in prison camps in Germany, to collaborate with or join the newly proclaimed Fascist Social Republic. Yet there has not been the necessary overall reevaluation of what occurred during those crucial weeks in September 1943. According to recent studies, about twenty thousand Italian military personnel lost their lives in the weeks following the armistice's proclamation, either in combat or at the hands of the Germans immediately after surrendering.[14] If to this we add those who, instead of going home, joined partisan units and those who refused to collaborate in German prison camps, a picture emerges that is quite different from the one that has hitherto inspired the totally negative judgment of the army's behavior and has regarded as more or less inevitable its humiliating dissolution at the time of the armistice.

A comprehensive scholarly study of the Italian armed forces in the aftermath of the armistice, free of the ideological bias that has made it difficult to understand this crucial episode of Italian history even today, would enable us to go beyond generic discussions of the country's moral crisis or the simple description of facts and individual culpability. The inadequacy and partiality of the existing studies oblige us to return to the documents and reread them from a fresh viewpoint. The Italian archival sources now accessible to scholars are of great help in clarifying essential aspects of the Italian exit from World War II.

The present study seeks to shed light on the negotiations between the Italians and Anglo-Americans, to clarify their respective objectives and to ascertain how the disaster that followed, the disintegration of the army and the German occupation, came about. My research required going beyond diplomatic history in order to understand the policies of the Italian leadership and the monarchy and to analyze the course of military events in Italy in light of the overall strategy of the Allies in the Mediterranean. The Italian army's condition and that of the people have remained in the background of this study, though they emerge more strongly at the end of the work. The population was a passive recipient of decisions made from above and was involved in a catastrophe whose causes it did not understand. In those days Italians, soldiers and civilians alike, had to make decisions without knowing their terms or their consequences, often without being able to distinguish the just from the unjust, with whom and against whom to side. If "tutti a casa" (let's all go home) was the response of most of the rank and file, the army's disintegration was due mainly to the failure of its commanders, who were unable or unwilling to organize resistance to the Germans.

A final question must be posed. If a clear order had been given to confront the Germans, would the country and the army have fought? While this is not the central focus of this book, I believe the time has come to establish what really happened in the aftermath of the armistice's proclamation. Without this it is impossible to understand whether the population's passivity was as total as portrayed in historical works and whether one can continue to speak of the two Italys, the resigned and apathetic one, which came to an end on September 8, and the active one, involved in the anti-Fascist resistance that came into being after the armistice.

The debts of gratitude I have incurred to institutions and archives are too numerous to list. Several friends and colleagues discussed controversial points with me concerning the armistice. They read parts of the manuscript and supported me during my work with affectionate solidarity. Above all, I would like to thank Gaetano Quagliariello and Victor Zaslavsky, who provided constant intellectual support and assisted me in many ways. I thank also Giuseppe

Introduction

Conti, to whom I turned for help with several problems concerning military aspects, Alessandro Clementi, Emilio Gentile, Luigi Goglia, Leonardo Musci and Luciano Zani for valuable suggestions and Roger Absalom, Volker Meja and Giovanni Orsina for help with revising the translation.

My greatest gratitude I reserve for the dean of Italian historiography, the late Renzo De Felice. Unknowingly, he was a constant interlocutor for me as I wrote this book. His opinion concerning September 8, 1943, was different from my own, as can be seen from his introduction to a companion volume containing a collection of documents on the Italian surrender I published for the Italian State Archives (Elena Aga-Rossi, *L'inganno reciproco. L'armistizio tra l'Italia e gli anglo-americani del settembre 1943*, with an introduction by Renzo De Felice, Rome: Ministero per i beni culturali e ambientali, 1993). The frequent conversations and friendly debates I had with him, however, stimulated me to verify and strengthen my arguments and to seek thoughtfully considered answers to problems that are still hotly debated among Italian historians and the public at large.

The first edition of this book was published in Italian in 1993, and the second, enlarged one in 1998, by the Il Mulino publishing house. For the present English edition, I have expanded some parts of the book, both to clarify situations and episodes little known to a non-Italian public and to place the Italian armistice in the context of Allied strategy. I did much of this work in September 1996, in an ideal setting, the beautiful Villa Serbelloni of the Rockefeller Foundation in Bellagio, where the courtesy of my hosts allowed me to study and write free of other concerns.

CHAPTER ONE

The Allies and Italy

FROM A SEPARATE PEACE TO UNCONDITIONAL SURRENDER

1. The First Formulations of British Strategy and the Role of Italy, "The Weakest Link of the Axis" (1940–41)

Italy entered the war in June 1940 at a time of intense stress for Great Britain, as the defeat at Dunkirk and the fall of France exposed it to a possible German invasion. Over the following months, British strategy was based on mobilizing existing resources, which were inadequate for offensive operations against the Axis powers and barely sufficient for maintaining a defensive position. In this situation, Great Britain attempted to create conditions for weakening the Axis countries, focusing on eroding their will to fight and undermining their morale by various means such as propaganda aimed at showing the inevitability of an Axis loss, air raids on their cities and naval blockades of their coasts. In this first phase, the British also relied on plans developed by the Special Operations Executive (SOE), the British secret service, to "set Europe ablaze," that is, to foment resistance and opposition movements within German-occupied countries by sending volunteers and weapons that were later to assist British liberating armies. The British placed enormous trust in the destructive effects of aerial bombardments, to the point of imagining the collapse of Germany and Italy, which would have made direct military action unnecessary. This optimistic view was expressed by Churchill in a July 1941 letter to Roosevelt, in which he described future British plans:

From a Separate Peace to Unconditional Surrender

> We have been considering here our war plans, not only for the
> fighting of 1942 but also for 1943.... In broad outline, we must
> aim first at intensifying the blockade and propaganda. Then, we
> must subject Germany and Italy to a ceaseless and ever growing air
> bombardment. These measures may themselves produce an internal
> convulsion or collapse. But plans ought also to be made for coming
> to the aid of the conquered populations by landing armies of liber-
> ation when opportunity is ripe.[1]

During the earlier period, therefore, offensive actions had to be
limited to the periphery, to the "soft underbelly" of the Axis, according to Churchill's well-known expression. During a second phase,
beginning in 1942, the British Empire would be in a position to "re-
enter the Continent" and attack Germany.[2] This is the context in
which British initiatives with respect to Italy during the first period
of the war must be placed.

The discussions of how to eliminate Italy from the war – it was
correctly regarded as "the weakest link"[3] of the Axis – had begun
within the British government immediately after Italy's entry into the
conflict. The British General Staff viewed this as a top priority and
prepared a series of plans that considered different possibilities, from
a separate peace to Italy's collapse. It is interesting that the analysis
of the situation and the plans to "knock Italy out of the war" with
heavy bombardment and intense propaganda remained nearly
unchanged from 1940 to 1943, in spite of changes in the military
situation.[4]

For a brief period between the end of 1940 and the beginning
of 1941, when Great Britain was fighting alone against Germany,
the overwhelming necessity of finding external support and the
initial failures of the Italian army – the disastrous campaign in
Greece, the destruction of the fleet at Taranto and the defeats
in Africa – induced the British government to examine the possibility of a separate peace with Italy.[5] Various scenarios for Italy
were examined, all of which were based on an overestimation
of opposition to the regime. They included Italy's defection from
the Axis, the emergence of active resistance to German occupation
and the transfer of part of the Italian fleet and air force to the

British. Trusting that the Fascist regime could be overthrown with suitable assistance, the British government discussed a series of initiatives, most suggested by the SOE. These ranged from the creation of a "Garibaldi legion," a voluntary army recruited from the Italian prisoners captured in Africa; to the establishment of a free Italian colony in Libya, which would receive the same treatment as the French colonies;[6] to a project for a clandestine landing of anti-Fascist militants in Sicily and Sardinia who would lay the groundwork for an Allied landing and form the "nucleus of a free Italy"; to the idea of inducing some naval commanders to turn over their ships for money or because of anti-Fascist ideals in exchange for a commitment to get their families out of Italy. In the first months of 1941, British agents committed various acts of sabotage in southern Italy.[7]

Churchill, who had just taken command of the British government, was among the strongest supporters of the attempt to disengage Italy from Germany. In this context, the December 1940 speech in which he declared that "one man alone," Mussolini, was responsible for the decision to enter the war, was a significant propaganda point and was also part of a plan to induce Italians to dissociate themselves from the regime.[8] In particular, Churchill enthusiastically supported the idea of a Garibaldi legion, which continued to be discussed throughout the spring of 1941.[9]

Stalin, too, ascribed great importance at that time to the possibility of Italy's collapse, according to the memoirs of British Foreign Minister Anthony Eden. During the British prime minister's visit to Moscow in December 1941, Stalin reportedly stated, "The weakest link of the Axis is Italy, and if this link is broken the whole Axis will collapse."[10]

However, Rommel's spring 1941 counteroffensive changed the military situation and dashed all hopes of Italy's departure from the war. Shortly thereafter, in June 1941, the German attack on the USSR closed the dramatic period of Great Britain's military isolation. From that moment on, it was increasingly less inclined to make concessions in exchange for Italy's withdrawal from the conflict.

2. The Allied Strategy in the Mediterranean: Military Objectives and Political Considerations

The entry of the United States into the war in December 1941 led to a radical change in Allied war aims. In contrast to the British strategy, which centered on the Mediterranean, the U.S. military strategy was based on a direct attack on the main enemy, the German Reich, through northern France, the shortest route. Once the objective had been defined, it was necessary to concentrate every effort on mobilizing forces for the attack, to be unleashed as soon as they were ready. The Americans initially excluded the opening of other secondary fronts in order to avoid delays in preparing for the landings in northern France.

With the abandonment of plans for operations in the Mediterranean, Italy was no longer of military interest, even if the Allied governments continued to discuss the possibility of its collapse – relying on the destructive psychological and physical effects of the air raids – or of a separate peace.

During 1942, two opposing views on the policy toward Italy were taking shape in the British government. The possibility of a separate peace increasingly lost interest for the Foreign Office and the War Cabinet. Only Churchill and the former supporters of "appeasement," such as the former foreign minister Samuel Hoare, now ambassador in Madrid, and the former ambassador in Rome, Percy Loraine, who by now were on the sidelines, continued to support the idea. The view of Foreign Minister Anthony Eden and the Foreign Office won out, and a "hard line" was adopted. This line was basically centered on one idea: the Italians had to realize that their alternative was "sinking or surviving." Any promises about Italy's future were therefore to be avoided.[11]

Eden in particular always demonstrated a special resentment toward the Italians and initiated a reversal of the policy pursued by Chamberlain to "appease the minor dictator," which in 1938 had led him to resign as foreign minister. Eden justified his opposition to a separate peace by stating that the Italian forces did not constitute a danger to the British and that, if they switched alliances,

Italy would not be in a position to make a meaningful military contribution.[12]

American policy concerning Italy developed along different lines. Beginning with tactics that almost amounted to courting the Fascist regime, in hopes of inducing it to make a separate peace, it evolved into the extreme position of demanding unconditional surrender and a complete purge of all Fascists, to be executed by the Allied military administration of the country. American policy toward the Fascist regime could be defined as an *appeasement* policy, keeping in mind, however, that the United States attributed little importance to Italy. The process that led the Roosevelt administration to assume an anti-Fascist attitude was a long one, and the eventual choice was more a result of Italy's alliance with Nazi Germany than based on the intrinsically antidemocratic nature of Fascism. In 1940, Roosevelt had tried to convince Mussolini to stay out of the conflict, both with direct appeals to the Duce personally and through emissaries. In 1939 he nominated Myron Taylor as his personal representative to the Holy See to establish a direct channel of communication through the Vatican. During his mission to Europe in the spring of 1940, Roosevelt's personal friend, Undersecretary of State Sumner Welles, visited Rome twice, but his talks with Italian leaders did not produce any tangible results. Having failed to obtain Italy's neutrality, Roosevelt began pushing Italy toward a separate peace. He continued to be convinced that the alliance between Italy and Germany was "unnatural," as he put it to Amleto Cicognani, apostolic delegate in Washington, shortly after his reelection in 1940. Roosevelt hoped that the American willingness to support Italy's territorial claims would induce Italy to leave the war. On several occasions, and even after the United States entered the war, Roosevelt communicated to Italian King Victor Emmanuel III that the American government continued to distinguish between Italy and Germany and had neither claims nor grudges against Italy. This conviction was due to several factors: the perception that the war was unpopular in Italy and therefore that Italy could be separated from the Axis; the lack of a clash of interests, which existed between Great Britain and Italy; and more important, the presence of an electorally important Italo-American community, which would have reacted unfavorably to an intransigent policy on Italy. This was the source of American willingness to favor a separate peace – which would have eliminated "the weakest link" of the Axis from the conflict – a willingness that lasted until June 1943 in spite of the official policy of unconditional surrender.[13]

This difference between the British and American policies regarding Italy was reflected in their relations with the anti-Fascist émigrés. The Foreign Office expressed the deepest mistrust and a total lack of interest in these émigrés and their cause. Unlike the State Department, which was in touch with such anti-Fascists as Max Ascoli, Carlo Sforza, Luigi Sturzo and even Gaetano Salvemini – although in a more turbulent fashion because of his intransigence – the Foreign Office distanced itself and pressured the American government not to recognize the anti-Fascist "Free Italy" movement or an Italian government in exile led by Sforza. Emilio Lussu, an anti-Fascist whose credentials were beyond reproach, since he had been founder and director with Carlo Rosselli of the "Justice and Liberty" movement, the most active anti-Fascist organization in exile, presented an offer to the British intelligence services in June 1942 to return to Italy to launch a guerrilla movement in Sardinia. He requested that, in return, the British government maintain Italy's territorial integrity, with the exception of some minor frontier changes. The Foreign Office decided without hesitation that it was not worth the effort.[14]

Lussu thought next of turning to the American government and sent his emissary, Dino Gentili, to the State Department with the same proposal. After a talk with Gentili, Assistant Secretary Adolph Berle asked the views of the British government on the suitability of a public statement showing a favorable Allied attitude toward Italy in accord with Gentili's request. Eden's reply of November 14, 1942, was decidedly negative:

> Question of desirability of making some political declaration to the Italian people on the lines suggested by the State Department is under urgent examination. As State Department will appreciate, the question bristles with difficulties. Pending examination we cannot commit ourselves to any promises to the Italian people, and I greatly

hope that nothing will be said in Washington which would prejudice our attitude or might suggest that the attitude of the United
States government is different from ours.

. . . Meanwhile line we are taking in political warfare is to inten-
sify anti-German feeling, stimulate the Italians to active as well as
passive resistance against the Fascist Party, stress that Italians want
peace, but to get it must organize active resistance against their
traitor government and its German masters.

. . . Even assuming that some political declaration were made,
it is essential in our view that it should be made to the Italian people,
and that we should not give any undertaking to, or enter into any
negotiations with, any Italian or group of Italians outside Italy. It
has always been the view of His Majesty's Government that any
liberating movement, or alternative Government, must come from
within the country itself. If we were successful in promoting any
internal upheaval in Italy (which would be the object of any declaration), an alternative Government might emerge from Italy itself.
It would then have proved highly inconvenient to have entered into
commitments with any leader or group outside Italy.

. . . Please explain position to the State Department. . . .[15]

Actually, Berle did not wait for the views of the Foreign Office,
but in a speech that was an indirect reply to Gentili's request, he
stated that the United States would safeguard the *Italian nationhood*
– a deliberately vague expression that indicated something halfway
between "sovereignty" and "territorial integrity."[16] Berle's speech
attracted some attention and was considered a position statement of
the American government. The *New York Times* editorialized that
the Italians did not identify themselves with their government as the
Germans did and that they therefore deserved greater consideration
from the Allies.[17]

At this point, Eden thought it best to clarify his own position in
a memorandum approved by the War Cabinet on November 20,
1942, in which he explained that an internal collapse followed by a
German occupation would be preferable to a separate peace. The
reason given was that Italy would thus become a burden for
Germany, while if it became an ally it could achieve an independent
position at the peace table. Eden argued as follows:

The limited objective of converting Italy into a definite liability to Germany may be from the military point of view of even greater value than the bigger objective of actually bringing Italy out of the war, since a neutral or even an Italy fighting on the Allied side could easily develop into a liability for the Allies, which might not be counterbalanced by the material and military benefits to be derived from such a situation. Up to the present Hitler has not had to expend much manpower on Italy; effective control of the country has been assured by the co-operation of the Fascist party, the presence of members of the Gestapo and the fact that one of the German air fleets made its headquarters in Italy, and German Army formations have from time to time passed through the country.

. . . In the event of an internal collapse, the Germans would have the choice either of abandoning Italy to her fate and making a frontier on the Brenner, or of sending troops to Italy to restore and possibly maintain the situation. Politically the Germans could not afford to accept the former alternative unless it were physically impossible for them to spare the troops necessary for an occupation of Italy.

. . . Furthermore, an internal collapse in Italy proper, especially if it led to or was proceeded [*sic*] by serious disaffection among the Italian armed forces, would probably result in a mutiny in the Italian forces of occupation in Greece, Yugoslavia and Albania. Thus the Germans would be forced to divert troops for the occupation of both Italy and the Balkans in order to take over the duties hitherto performed by Italy in the Balkans. An occupation of Italy and the Balkans would require thirty to forty divisions.

. . . A German occupation of Italy would be intensely distasteful to the Italian people, would greatly increase unrest in the country and should predispose the population in our favour and thus facilitate any military operations on our own part against Italy.[18]

This choice reflected a long-term political goal with respect to Italy. The Foreign Office meant to impose a punitive peace that would prevent any future Italian government from making requests concerning Italy's territorial integrity or the maintenance of the colonies and eventually once again threatening British power in the Mediterranean. Churchill voiced his dissent a few days later, in a note on the "Position of Italy":

It is in my opinion premature to assume that no internal convulsion in Italy could produce a Government which would make a separate peace.... [T]he Italian people will have to choose between, on the one hand, setting up a Government under someone like Grandi to sue for a separate peace, or, on the other, submitting to a German occupation, which would merely aggravate the severity of the war.[19]

Thus, the British prime minister declared himself in favor of pursuing a separate peace in order to avoid the grave consequences of a German occupation of Italy, although he agreed with Eden on the "bombardment strategy" and the appropriateness of not accepting conditions from the defeated. His position, however, remained a minority view. Eden in any event acted on the reference to Grandi. On December 2, 1942, he sent Churchill a summary of Italian initiatives to sound out the British government on a separate peace. He stated, "I have decided against pursuing any of these contacts," but made an exception for Grandi: "We can consider these requests if and when we see signs of an alternative government emerging under someone like Grandi ready to make peace with us and resist the Germans."[20]

At Eden's suggestion, the War Cabinet decided that "no special importance was to be attached" to any of the approaches made at that time by Italians. The Cabinet adopted all Eden's reservations on an Italian request for separate peace as its own:

(a) There would be great military advantage to us in bringing Italy out of the war. It had been suggested that such a development would involve us in additional military commitments. If, however, Italy were to seek a separate peace and then ask for our military assistance against Germany, it did [sic] not follow that we would automatically be under an obligation to provide such help. We should be careful to avoid committing ourselves in advance; our decision on such an appeal would be made at the time in the light of circumstances as they then stood.

(b) The United States Government were very anxious to bring Italy out of the war; and were already following a vigorous policy directed to that end. If, as was the case, we were in sympathy with their ultimate objective in this matter, we should not leave the initiative too much to them but should keep the closest contact with them in the prosecution of this policy. The difficulties which had arisen with Darlan's position in North Africa were quoted as an illustration of the importance of maintaining close liaison with the United States Government in such matters.

(c) Some apprehension was expressed as to the political consequences of entertaining overtures for a separate peace if they should be made by persons who had formerly been prominently associated with Fascist Party and régime. Those sections of public opinion which regarded this war as primarily a war to end Fascism would view with suspicion anything which could be represented as a compromise with Fascist elements.

On the other hand it was pointed out that our primary war aim was the destruction of German Nazism and the restoration of the countries whose territories had been over-run. If at a time of internal upheaval in Italy an individual seized power and came forward with an offer to conclude a separate peace, then, if we were satisfied that he could bring Italy out of the war and that this would give us a substantial military advantage in reaching our primary objective, we would not be justified in declining to negotiate merely on the ground of his political record. We should not tie our hands in advance regarding the type of Italian Government with which we would be prepared to negotiate a separate peace: that decision must be taken at the time on the basis of a realistic appraisal of the practical advantages and disadvantages involved.

(d) Meanwhile, however, no suggestion would be made that we shall be prepared in certain circumstances to have dealings with particular individuals (e.g. Grandi), whose names were already being mentioned in certain circles. There would be no attempt to build up any potential opponent of the present Fascist regime. We must await developments and see what alternative leaders might emerge, so that we might remain entirely free to take advantage of any opportunity which might present itself.[21]

The contorted style of this memorandum points to the ambiguity and unresolved contradictions in the British position. Having discouraged initiatives by the Italian anti-Fascists, the British government remained receptive to the idea of signing a separate peace with an Italian government headed by Grandi. As Bruce Lockhart noted with alarm in his diary, the prime minister was "playing with the idea of Italian Darlans."[22] On the other hand, the negative reaction of public opinion to the Darlan deal was too close not to cause fears that it would recur in the Italian case as well.[23] It is important to recognize, however, that Eden's decidedly intransigent attitude toward a separate peace with Italy gradually prevailed and became the official British government position *before* the Allied decision to adopt the principle of unconditional surrender.

As has been shown, the United States was initially much more disposed and even favorable to a separate peace with Italy, but the U.S. attitude became less accommodating after "the Darlan affair" and the serious Italian setbacks in the fall of 1942.

3. The Adoption of the Unconditional Surrender Principle at the Casablanca Conference

The determining role of the Foreign Office in deciding policy on Italy was sanctioned by the adoption of the unconditional surrender principle formulated by Roosevelt and Churchill at the Casablanca Conference, which was held from January 12 to 26, 1943, and then approved by Stalin.

Italy's surrender constituted the first application of this principle that was to guide Allied policy until the end of the war.

The adoption of the unconditional surrender principle was proclaimed by Roosevelt in an almost casual way at a press conference that took place at the end of the meeting. Both Roosevelt and Churchill later emphasized the improvised, even accidental nature of the decision. Roosevelt told his friend and confidant Harry Hopkins that "the thought popped into my head,"[24] while Churchill, speaking to the House of Commons on July 21, 1949, remembered that he heard the expression for the first time when Roosevelt pronounced it at the press conference.

This account of how the decision was reached to impose unconditional surrender on the Axis countries is not in accord with investigations by historians, who have arrived at entirely different conclusions: the decision was neither spontaneous nor casual; rather, unconditional surrender was a policy set in advance and previously elaborated. Roosevelt was not the first to use the expression. It is likely that "unconditional surrender" was mentioned for the first time in a meeting of the Subcommittee on Security Problems, appointed by the State Department back in May 1942. The subcommittee concluded that "unconditional surrender rather than an armistice should be sought from the principal enemies, Germany and Japan, except perhaps Italy."[25] Roosevelt had been informed of these conclusions. Therefore, the State Department had come out in favor of unconditional surrender long before the Casablanca Conference. There were conflicting positions both among the military and within the State Department. The secretary of state in particular notes in his memoirs that he was against unconditional surrender, because he feared that its adoption could "prolong the war, turning Axis resistance into a state of desperation." His position was widely shared then and later.[26]

With some exceptions, the American military was favorable to the extension of the unconditional surrender principle to Italy. The earliest draft of Italy's surrender has never been published or examined by historians. Prepared in May 1942 by General George V. Strong and reviewed in September 1942 by the State Department, it regarded unconditional surrender as a purely military act, involving an agreement between the commander in chief of the Italian armed forces and that of the United Nations. It is not clear in the draft what the attitude toward the Italian government was to be. The first paragraph defines the "surrender terms":

> The Commander in Chief of the Italian Armed Forces agrees to unconditional surrender to the Commander in Chief of the United Nations Armed Forces, or his representative, and to the cessation of hostilities on land, sea and air within a period of twelve hours, and to abide by the conditions hereinafter set forth in these terms of surrender.[27]

A document of November 1942 prepared by the State Department's Subcommittee on Security Problems of the Advisory Committee on Foreign Relations, chaired by Harley Notter, was much more precise. The document announced the principles to be applied to the occupation of Italy, in the likely event that "the hostilities [were] terminated by the unconditional surrender of the enemy": from the attribution of "absolute authority" to the military commander, to "indirect rule," that is, leaving as much as possible to local administration. The problem of whether to recognize an Italian national government was to be decided by the United Nations.

Since these principles were faithfully applied after the armistice, with the unforeseen variant of the German occupation of a large part of Italian territory, the central part of the document is given here:

> It is the anticipation of the United Nations that hostilities will be terminated by the unconditional surrender of the enemy. This will be followed, in the case of Italy, by the military occupation of the country. The following principles are considered as applicable to such occupation:
>
> 1. Italy should be occupied by a mobile force of moderate size, stationed at strategic centers throughout the country but with full power to move freely wherever necessary.
> 2. This force should be unified under a single command and should be composed of American and British forces operating in the European theater.
> 3. While the broad policies of the occupation administration will be formulated by the United Nations political authorities, the military commander should within the scope of those policies have absolute authority over the occupied territory.
> 4. The military commander should have the power to issue decrees, to set up courts, to exercise the police power and to remove local officials who do not cooperate loyally with his administration. He should, however, permit satisfactory local officials, courts and police to continue, under appropriate supervision, their normal duties, insofar as these are compatible with the purposes of the occupation.

5. Whether or not an Italian national government shall be recognized and, if so, the degree of authority which should at various states of the occupation be accorded to that government will be determined by the United Nations political authorities in consultation with the military commander.[28]

In December 1942, the Joint Chiefs of Staff suggested that no armistice be offered to Germany, Japan, Italy or their satellite countries until they had accepted the "unconditional surrender" of their armed forces. In a January 7, 1943, meeting with the Joint Chiefs of Staff, before his departure for the Casablanca Conference, the U.S. president repeated his intention of bringing up the idea of "unconditional surrender" as the basis of American objectives.[29]

Churchill too, in his memoirs, altered his earlier statements that he had not been informed of Roosevelt's intentions regarding unconditional surrender. During the conference, Roosevelt raised with Churchill the question of whether unconditional surrender should be adopted in the Italian case. The two leaders had thought to apply this principle to Japan and Germany and to exclude Italy in order to "encourage a break-up" within that country – that is, the possibility of a separate peace, which both men continued to pursue. Churchill informed the War Cabinet telegraphically, asking for its opinion. The answer, formulated by Eden and Attlee, made clear the disagreement on Italy that divided the British government. The War Cabinet approved the adoption of unconditional surrender, but strongly opposed the exclusion of Italy, maintaining that it would be "a mistake to make a distinction among the three Axis partners," because the threat of severe and intransigent treatment would create a better possibility of obtaining "the desired effect on Italian morale"[30] than would a soft attitude. Eden's line of anticipating not a separate peace with Italy but its occupation by the Germans thus became the basis for Allied strategy concerning Italy, in spite of the contrary view of Churchill and Roosevelt.

There is no doubt, however, that the idea of unconditional surrender was always connected primarily to the name of Roosevelt and reflected his policy. In his speeches and public appeals, Roosevelt often emphasized the need to pursue total and complete victory, without making compromises with the aggressor states, in sharp contrast to his actual diplomatic activities.[31] One of his most perceptive biographers, Robert Sherwood, wrote that the unconditional surrender strategy was "very deeply deliberated" and reflected a "considered policy" on Roosevelt's part.[32] Anne Armstrong, in a work dedicated to the issue of unconditional surrender, added that this formula reflected "a basic American attitude toward the enemy, toward international politics and toward war."[33]

The principle of unconditional surrender transformed the war into a moral crusade. With this formula, Roosevelt made himself the interpreter of the outrage that Americans directed against aggressors, in the first place Germany and Japan. It was a proclamation that the United States would not be satisfied with less than total victory and that no chances for a negotiated peace between the Allies and the Axis countries existed at all. The objectives of the war thus included the total destruction of Axis military power – "the smashing of militarism" in Roosevelt's words – and a thorough punishment of war criminals in the enemy states. Not only would the defeated aggressors be demilitarized, but strong measures would be taken to prevent rearmament in Germany, Japan and Italy, whose peoples must be "taught a lesson," so that it would be "necessary for them to earn their way back into the fellowship of peace-loving and law-abiding nations."[34]

The first question to be answered is, what was Roosevelt trying to achieve in proclaiming the principle of unconditional surrender? The idea of being protagonists in a struggle between good and evil, between Fascism and anti-Fascism, between liberators and usurpers that would continue until the forces of evil were destroyed had an enormous influence on public opinion both in occupied Europe and among the combatants. The soldiers of the Allied forces felt called on to fight for a just cause, for the liberation of oppressed peoples in totalitarian regimes. They were thus united by an ideal common to the internal opponents in the separate occupied countries. The principle of unconditional surrender summed all that up and became an effective formula of Allied propaganda, in contrast to the "total war" promoted at the same time by Goebbels. The proclamation of the unconditional surrender principle was meant to overcome criticisms of the American government that had ensued from the Darlan affair. On the other hand, in choosing to impose unconditional surrender on the enemy powers, the "domestic" goal of strengthening the Allied coalition certainly prevailed over the "external" one of preventing any compromise and destroying Nazism and Fascism.

The main objective was to reassure the Soviet Union of the will of the Western governments to continue until the total defeat of Germany.[35] In his first public statements on his return from Casablanca, Roosevelt refuted the rumors started by Nazi propaganda according to which the alliances among regimes as different as the democratic Western governments and the Soviet Union were destined to break up.[36] With the adoption of the unconditional surrender principle, Roosevelt and Churchill asked the USSR to make a commitment not to stipulate a separate peace with Germany. This was a real possibility at that time, when relations among the three leaders were very tense because of the Western delay in opening a second front and when Stalin had even refused to meet Roosevelt and Churchill. The principle was thus to serve as a binding force between the three great Allied powers, in lieu of political agreements for the postwar period, on which they were never to achieve identical positions.

The military situation in January 1943 was still very serious, and only in the following months was it clear that the victories at Stalingrad and in Africa represented a turning point in the war. However, a separate peace between the Soviet Union and Germany would have been lethal for the outcome of the war. Many critics of the unconditional surrender principle have maintained that the fears expressed by Allied leaders of a separate peace between the USSR and Germany were groundless because "Russia could not quit" the war and Hitler could not be induced to make peace with the Soviets.[37] It might be objected that such criticisms inappropriately assume total coherence in Hitler's wartime conduct and reveal an ignorance of Stalin's historical experience and motivations. It was clarified several years ago that the fears of the Western governments were based on accurate information, such as that obtained from intercepted Japanese telegrams.[38] As for the Soviets, the documents made available in the archives after the collapse of the USSR have confirmed the thesis advanced by some historians that during the end of 1942 and the beginning of 1943 – the period when Roosevelt decided to adopt the principle of unconditional surrender – the Soviets were engaged in a series of moves toward the German leadership to achieve a separate peace. It is now also known that from the beginning of the German attack, Stalin had tried to reach a compromise peace with Hitler.[39]

It is therefore understandable why Roosevelt intended to prevent Russia from leaving the war with a formula that presented a goal common to the three Allied powers and justified the American decision not to discuss territorial questions, at least not officially, on which the Allied powers disagreed.

On the other hand, no declaration could have overcome the Soviets' deep distrust of the Anglo-Americans or prevented them from seeking alternative solutions, if these appeared more favorable to Soviet interests. The unconditional surrender proclamation did not prevent Stalin from continuing to explore a possible separate peace with Germany, even in the spring and summer of 1943.

This is perhaps why the Soviet government did not react to the Anglo-American initiative and did not even acknowledge its existence between late January and early May 1943. The term simply was not present either in official statements or in Stalin's letters to Roosevelt or Churchill. Only after several months did this formula begin to appear in official statements, beginning with Stalin's speech of May 1 in which he insisted that "only a total defeat of Hitler's army and the unconditional surrender of Hitler's Germany could lead to establishing peace in Europe."[40] Although he used the expression when he thought it appropriate, Stalin never felt committed to the principle of unconditional surrender and did not hesitate to set it aside whenever the issue at hand was that of getting Axis satellites out of the war. In fact, the armistices with the Eastern European countries signed by Russia and accepted by the United States and Great Britain were negotiated and included territorial changes. The Soviet dictator also expressed the view that it would be better to tell the Germans what they could expect from unconditional surrender, establishing exact terms. In particular, at the Teheran Conference, held from November 29 to December 1, 1943, Stalin argued that unconditional surrender seemed "bad tactics vis-à-vis Germany," suggesting that the Allies draft the conditions and make them known to the German people.[41] Roosevelt, on the other hand, showed himself completely opposed to defining exact surrender terms, because there was the risk that such a definition would "omit or leave open for discussion some other conditions that are now or that may in the future become of equal importance from our point of view," but especially because a surrender "on terms" would signify a repetition of Wilson's errors.[42]

In fact, it was obvious from the beginning that the concept of unconditional surrender had different meanings for each of the three leaders and that their governments tried to impose their own viewpoint every time the disagreement emerged. Italy constituted the acid test both for applying the principle and for settling the differences between contrasting viewpoints.

In Italy's case, the unconditional surrender principle dominated the political debate between the British and American governments. The discussion centered on how the principle was to be implemented and what the consequences would be if Italy requested capitulation. One controversial aspect was whether the formula implied the elimination only of the Fascist regime or of the monarchy as well. Roosevelt raised the question officially in a memorandum prepared at his request by the State Department in May 1943 to serve as a basis for discussing future policy toward Italy. Pursuant to the line followed until then – that is, to leave open the possibility of a move by the monarchy to take Italy out of the Axis – the position of the State Department on the monarchy was an open one:

> The prerogatives of the Crown should be considered as suspended. The moral power of the Crown among the Italian people and the army may require some special treatment of this question as the situation develops.[43]

In reviewing the text, Roosevelt accepted the first sentence and canceled the rest, assuming a much more clear-cut attitude on the monarchy question.

The British in that period were posing the same question. In a long memorandum prepared in March 1943 by the historian John Wheeler-Bennett and discussed by the Foreign Office in May, the monarchy was among Italy's future problems under discussion:

> In the first place it must be decided whether the formula of "unconditional surrender" is to be interpreted to mean that not only the Fascist regime, but also the House of Savoy must be eliminated from the Italian scene before a cessation of hostilities is agreed to. If a deposition is decided on it must be with some idea of what alternative regime is desired.[44]

In sending Wheeler-Bennett's memorandum from Washington to the Foreign Office, Sir Ronald Campbell, minister at the British Embassy in Washington, stressed that it did not represent the opinion of the Embassy, and certainly the prevailing position in the British government was in favor of retaining the monarchy. In any event, the document illustrates the debate within the British government on the attempt to apply the principle of unconditional surrender.

The same question was to be posed with regard to retaining the emperor when the Japanese surrender was under discussion.

The most immediate issue before the American and British governments in the spring of 1943, however, was that of drafting an instrument of surrender to be imposed on Italy in case it decided to capitulate. The attention given the issue brought out the difference between the two governments' understanding of the meaning of unconditional surrender. Roosevelt understood it as a way to make a tabula rasa of the enemy, refusing to recognize whatever government might be in power at that moment and imposing a military administration on that part of its territory which military requirements would have made it necessary to occupy. All authority was to be transferred to the commander in chief of the Allied forces, to whom the commander in chief of the Italian armed forces was to surrender. This position had been agreed upon before the Casablanca

Conference, so that the principle of unconditional surrender simply provided a justification for it. Roosevelt in particular did not intend to make any political commitment to persons or groups in Italy and other countries the Allies might occupy – and actually he assumed the same attitude toward France as well, refusing to recognize de Gaulle's Free French Committee. In a conversation with Eden in March 1943 during the latter's visit to Washington, with Secretary of State Cordell Hull and Harry Hopkins present, he stated that he did not want a "negotiated armistice after the collapse. . . . [W]e should insist on total surrender with no commitments to the enemy as to what we would or would not do after this action."

The United States, insisting on a purely military surrender, meant to distinguish a first phase, when every decision would be delegated to the military, from a second phase, in which the Allies would take up the political questions and face the problem of governing the occupied country. This attitude was unrealistic because, as has already been noted, "a surrender agreement is essentially a political bargain. To aim at obtaining surrender while ruling out bargaining on principle is a contradiction in terms."[45] But throughout the war, the U.S. government attempted to show to the American public that its objectives were purely military and had nothing to do with European political questions. When the problem of the German surrender came up, Roosevelt adopted the same position he had taken in the Italian and French cases. In summing up a conversation he had with Roosevelt in September 1944, Robert Murphy wrote:

> The President also expressed the view that it might be better for the Allies in concluding hostilities with the Germans to deal only with local commanders and authorities, rather than with a central authority and the German high command. This, he indicated, would protect us from the charge of having made a deal with anybody or to have become affiliated with a group which, while pretending to be anti-Nazi, might be a cover for unwelcome elements.[46]

On the Italian armistice the British government's position was totally different. According to the British, the political problem could not be put off and the two governments needed to fix precise surrender conditions to be imposed on Italy. From December 1942 on, a commission on reconstruction impaneled by the Foreign Office, the Law Commission, had met to discuss the surrender text. In April 1943 it completed a document with thirty-nine articles, which, after having been discussed and amended by the government with the addition of new articles, bringing their number to forty-four, was transmitted to the Americans in June. With further small amendments but never-ending discussions, it was later to become the "long armistice."[47] The document was to be used if Italy were to request an armistice while the war with Germany was still going on, and it contained some political and economic clauses in addition to the military surrender terms.

A hardening of the British government's position is clear between the first draft in April and the June version. In no way could the first version be characterized as demanding unconditional surrender. That version in fact granted the "honors of war" (Article 3) to the Italian armed forces, that is, the retention of swords and pistols by officers and of small arms and side arms by soldiers of lower rank, a point later omitted. The first version also mentioned "the demobilization of the excess Italian armed forces" (Article 13) and the order to assemble the warships in ports to be specified later by the United Nations (Article 6, later 7), to which was added subsequently, "Some ships can be used under United Nations command," the implication being that the rest of the fleet would remain under Italian authority. Finally, there was no mention of the costs of occupation, which in later versions were charged to the Italian government. In the final document, Italian sovereignty over its own territory was suspended. It is likely that the toughening of the surrender conditions was a consequence of the decline in Italy's military situation and of the final defeat in Africa during this period. Both versions of the armistice terms prepared by the British government assumed the existence of a government or central authority that would sign and respect the "articles of surrender." This was the point where the opposing views of the two Allied governments on unconditional surrender clashed in a long and agonizing confrontation.

From a Separate Peace to Unconditional Surrender

The Joint Chiefs of Staff rejected the British text sent to Washington because it did not amount to unconditional surrender and contradicted the official policy announced by the two governments. Instead, they proposed applying the directive published for establishing a military government in Sicily, with some corrections, accompanied by a "Proclamation to the Italian People," in which General Eisenhower would be proclaimed "Military Governor of Metropolitan Italy."[48]

The long discussion between the two governments on the content of the surrender document illustrates the different approaches to the problem of occupying an enemy country, which was to arise again in the case of Germany. A clear statement of the American view can be found in the draft for the German surrender prepared in January 1944, in which any negotiations were ruled out. The enemy nation would have to declare itself defeated and "ready to submit without question to any terms of military, political, economic and territorial nature which may be imposed on it by the victor."[49]

In the Italian case, the Americans accused the British of intending to "negotiate" with the enemy government, which would be left in place, instead of imposing unconditional surrender. Roosevelt was disturbed by the use of the word "armistice" rather than "terms of surrender."[50] In a lengthy note of July 12, Eden summed up the differences between British and Americans "(a) for the unconditional surrender of Italy, and (b) for the Administration to be set up in the country after the surrender."[51] The disagreement on the first point was that

> [t]he Americans take the line that it would be impossible to sign "articles of surrender" on the lines of our draft with any Italian Government and that their conception is that the King or the head of the Government or the Italian supreme military commander, preferably all three, should be forced to sign a broad acknowledgement of unconditional surrender, an essential feature of which would be the abdication of the King and the disappearance of the head of the Government immediately after, and a transfer of all powers to the Allies.[52]

On the second point, the disagreement concerned the powers of the supreme commander. According to the Americans the supreme commander could decide on the surrender and impose an Allied administration, whereas the British believed that such a decision had to be referred to the governments, as did the question of whether to extend the military government to all of Italy. Further, Eden maintained that his government had no intention of *negotiating* an armistice, but only of imposing one on the Italian government, which, if it remained in power, would free the Allies from "the whole burden of administering and maintaining order in Italy."[53]

The discussion took place on the theoretical plane as well. The American government held that there should not be even any mention of "armistice," but only of "unconditional surrender" or "surrender terms." The British government resorted to a legal argument to reply that an armistice did not necessarily imply negotiations and that in any case

> [a]n Armistice is necessarily a *negotiated* instrument. It can be wholly dictated and imposed on the enemy in consequence of his total defeat and request for a cessation of hostilities. Therefore, there is nothing in the signature of an Armistice or equivalent instrument which is incompatible with the enemy's "unconditional surrender." It should, indeed, be the best method of making the fact of that surrender plain and placing it on permanent record with the enemy's signed admission of it.[54]

After months of dispute, the two governments arrived at a compromise: the British removed the word "armistice" from the first draft of April 1943 and replaced it with "terms of surrender," and the Americans, after many protests about the usefulness of a document that claimed to contain everything, accepted the British version.

4. The Failure of Italian Attempts to Reach a Separate Peace

The Italian defeats in Africa and Russia in the second half of 1942 reinforced a hard line among the Allies against granting any concessions to Italy. On the other hand, these defeats, especially the one at El Alamein, led to a series of timid attempts by the Italians to establish contact with the Allied forces.

There is now an extensive literature on the various Italian moves to sound out Allied intentions regarding an eventual separate peace,[55] so that it is not necessary to retell the history of the different Italian emissaries. We will instead limit ourselves to indicating their objectives and comparing them with those of the Allied governments. In general, nearly all the promoters of these overtures belonged to the elite of the Italian regime and were led to take action by the increasingly widespread realization that Italy was on its way to catastrophe. Most of these initiatives, though independent of each other, came from circles connected to the monarchy. Throughout this period, the Italians turned to England on the unfounded assumption that the British would be more favorable to the monarchy and because of the greater ease in resuming contacts in place before Italy's decision to enter the war on Germany's side. Even when an opportunity arose to establish direct contact with the U.S. government during the period between Mussolini's ouster and Italy's surrender, it was allowed to lapse.[56]

The only information on some of these overtures can be found in the British archives, not in the Italian ones. According to the British intelligence services, Badoglio attempted to establish contact with the British from May 1942 on,[57] but there is no confirmation from Badoglio or other sources, even though he was considered in Italy to be the most likely successor to Mussolini in case of a military coup. The names of others who approached the British are those of Duke Aimone d'Aosta, General Enrico Caviglia and other lesser actors. A special case is that of the Princess Maria José, wife of Crown Prince Umberto, who turned to Salazar, Prime Minister of Portugal, as mediator. She persuaded him to plead the Italian cause directly to the British on the eve of the July 25 meeting of the Fascist Grand Council, which overthrew Mussolini.[58]

With the intensification of air raids on industrial centers and large cities in the north during the early months of 1943, and with the defeats in Africa, the belief that the war was lost was gaining ground. Meetings became frequent between regime leaders and the opposition to seek a way out of the conflict, but the prevailing sentiment was one of impotence.

The fragility of the moves undertaken in this period was due to the fact that none of those who promoted them could really speak in the name of the king. Victor Emmanuel III was "weak, undecided and excessively . . . deferential to the Government of the Hon. Mussolini."[59] He allowed several people to harbor hopes of his intervention to release Italy from Germany, but he did not take any action. It is probable that the king continued to delude himself about Italy's military potential, convinced that the Italian army would resist in case of an Anglo-American landing. In a conversation with Dino Grandi on June 4, 1943, the sovereign expressed the view that "our troops will resist and fight. We still have enough time to bring decisions to fruition which . . . we will take at the appropriate time."[60] The king underestimated Allied military power, held the British and Americans in contempt and showed no interest in the proposal to establish contacts for a separate peace before Mussolini's dismissal.[61]

General Vittorio Ambrosio, who had replaced Cavallero in February 1943 as chief of the General Staff, also underestimated Allied power and the seriousness of the Italian military situation, as we will see. As to the domestic situation, Pietro Acquarone, minister of the Royal Household and one of the few who could interpret the king's intentions, mentioned Badoglio as Mussolini's probable successor and opined that there would be no problems, either with the Fascist hierarchs "ready to dismiss Mussolini" or with the anti-Fascists – "there were hardly any" – and that the country would rally around the monarchy.[62]

As to Mussolini's position, it is difficult to say whether the Italian unconditional surrender prevented a direct attempt on his part or on the part of those close to him to achieve a separate peace. Mussolini may have shared the widespread opinion that any moves by persons closely tied to Fascism would be rejected, but that position had no resonance in the British government.[63]

It is important to note, on the other hand, that up to the last moment Mussolini tended toward a separate peace, not with the

Anglo-Americans, but with the Soviet Union, so that the Axis could concentrate all its forces on the Mediterranean. He tried repeatedly to convince Hitler that this would be the best solution. Between the end of 1942 and the beginning of 1943, this plan had some basis for support and constituted one of the greatest concerns of the Anglo-Americans, but it was less likely after the Soviet victories in the winter and spring of 1943, culminating in the Battle of Kursk in July. This solution had its supporters within the Third Reich as well, but it encountered an insuperable obstacle in Hitler. In February 1943, at the time of the shake-up in Mussolini's government, von Hassel commented:

> But would there still be anyone to make peace with Mussolini? Perhaps. Certainly not with Hitler, with the exception of Stalin – but this could be done only at the cost of completely relinquishing any German claims on Russian territory or influence, and Hitler could hardly do this.[64]

The idea of a separate peace between Germany and the USSR continued to dominate Mussolini's plans, so much so that barely four hours before his arrest he asked Japanese Ambassador Hidaka for his government's mediation. Even after the fall of Mussolini, both the Italian government and the Anglo-Americans considered the idea of a separate peace with the USSR to be possible.[65]

It is known that Foreign Ministry Undersecretary Giuseppe Bastianini was pressuring Mussolini first to find a way to get Italy out of the conflict, in conjunction with the Hungarians and Romanians, and later to establish contact with the Anglo-Americans. The Duce did not directly take any action but allowed Bastianini to proceed on his own.[66] Bastianini's initiatives were as complex as they were unreal, because they assumed German acceptance of a separate peace between the satellite states and the Anglo-Americans.[67]

Some Fascist leaders moved without Mussolini's knowledge. Dino Grandi tried at first to aim for a "constitutional crisis" in promoting the coup of July 25. He hoped that the king would accept an immediate reversal of alliances as soon as Mussolini was out of the picture and that he would be the king's spokesman before the

British government.[68] Even Ciano tried to make contact with the British. It is likely that Mussolini was reluctant to request a separate peace from the Anglo-Americans since that would be a "betrayal" of his ally, but at the same time he was the only one with the power and the capacity to take the initiative. According to Grandi, "the Fascist leaders were prisoners of Mussolini just like the anti-Fascists confined in the islands."[69]

The anti-Fascists, especially those living abroad, tried to establish contacts with both the British and the Americans in order to find a solution to the Italian crisis, but with few results. The most concrete attempt, that of Lussu, has already been discussed. Within the Mazzini Society, an organization of anti-Fascists in the United States during World War II, there was an attempt to create a volunteer force. However, the anti-Fascist attempts at collaboration generally did not get beyond the planning stage. In Italy, representatives of the Action Party deluded themselves into thinking that they could establish a democratic alternative to the palace coup that was taking form. However, the British government showed no interest in closer contacts with this group of anti-Fascists.[70]

Actually, for the British, the principle of unconditional surrender justified the intransigent posture adopted previously. British officials, especially Eden, decided not to respond to any of the overtures made by Italians in neutral countries, because, as we have seen, they did not want to make any agreements with an Italian government, but preferred to aim for Italy's total defeat. However, there was no ideological prejudice against personalities of the Fascist regime. Indeed, the only name the British government was willing to consider was that of Grandi.

During this period, the British government and the Foreign Office in particular were nearly able to monopolize contacts with the Italians, thanks to the American decision to leave European affairs to the British. Further, the Foreign Office not only blocked every move, but tried to prevent the Italian emissaries from turning to the Americans for fear that they would be more receptive.

Given the dominant British viewpoint and the Italians' lack of determination, it can be concluded that from the middle of 1942 to the fall of Mussolini in July 1943 there was no concrete possibility of achieving a separate peace between Italy and the Allies.

The British documents show that the Foreign Office continued to count on the possibility of Italy's internal collapse rather than on diplomatic negotiations. This forecast was supported by reports from several sources, especially British intelligence, on the deterioration of the Italian people's morale, on an increasing weariness with a war they regarded by then as lost and on the defeatism then spreading even in the army.

The collapse of Italy was to be brought about by continuous air raids – the Soviets were also stressing their advantageous effects[71] – and by a propaganda campaign to convince the Italians that an Allied victory was inevitable. A document presented at Casablanca optimistically predicted that Italy's collapse would be followed by a German withdrawal to northern Italy. However, in this case, it was proposed that the Allies not intervene. "We should not assume any obligation for the defense and full occupation of Italy since: ... We should encounter insuperable difficulties in conducting operations against the Germans established in a strong, natural defensive position in the Alps."[72]

5. Disagreements between the British and Americans on Military Strategy for the Mediterranean: From the Casablanca Conference to the Landing in Sicily

In facing the problem of defeating the Axis powers, the British and American governments held substantially different assumptions and strategic objectives. The British favored limited attacks of Axis forces on the periphery, while the Americans were pushing for a direct attack on Germany through northern France. During the war, the plans initially drawn up by the alliance underwent continual changes in response to the general situation, the growing weight of the Soviet Union in the war against Germany and Stalin's capacity to influence the choices of his Western Allies. First the landing in Sicily and later the Italian campaign represented decisions that had not been foreseen in the Allies' initial plans, but emerged as the result of a kind of double compromise between the British and American strategies on the one hand and between the contrasting Soviet and Western positions on opening a second front on the other.

The first Anglo-American military plans for the Mediterranean were quite different from what the Italians supposed. In the Allied strategy for 1943, Italy had a decidedly secondary place. It was only at the Casablanca Conference in January 1943 that an attack on Sicily was chosen to be the next step in the Allied offensive, a decision that was to carry great weight for Italy's future. The landing in Sicily was proposed by the British and accepted by Roosevelt in spite of strenuous opposition from American military commanders. Churchill was able to convince Roosevelt that such an operation was appropriate because it would bring on the fall of the Fascist regime, take Italy out of the war and keep the German Army busy in a diversionary action since the landing in Normandy could not be carried out in 1943.

Another objective was not officially recognized but, as has been seen, was clearly present for the Americans from the end of 1942, namely that of preventing the Soviet Union, left alone to fight the Germans, from deciding on a separate peace with Hitler. It was at this time that Clark Kerr, British ambassador in Moscow, warned that "if we do not form a second front in Europe this summer Russia would make a separate peace."[73]

As a result, the forces assigned to the Mediterranean were limited from the beginning, since some of them had been allocated to the preparation of the landing in Normandy, the code name for which was Overlord. The landing was prepared amid uncertainty and danger, to which was added a profound sense among the Allies of their own weakness. There was a crisis of indecision as early as the beginning of April, when Eisenhower, as Allied supreme commander for the Mediterranean, sent a telegram to the Joint Chiefs of Staff stating that the presence of two German divisions in Sicily put the landing there in danger.[74] Up to the eve of the operation, Eisenhower continued to express his fears about a long battle for control of the island.[75] Military preparations were accompanied by a massive propaganda operation and a series of diversions to attract the Germans' attention to other objectives.[76]

The decision to land in Sicily brought with it the problem of what kind of occupation should be imposed on Italy. Up to that moment, the United States had delegated the management of Italian political affairs to the British. In the spring of 1943, the Americans began to change their position of substantial detachment from Italian domestic matters. The initial disagreements between the two governments began then: who was to be the "senior partner" with the greater responsibility for governing Italy, and whether there would be a direct administration, with the elimination of the Fascist bureaucracy, or an indirect one, with the partical participation of this bureaucracy.[77]

The Foreign Office decisively opposed the increasingly insistent proposals from the Special Operations Executive and the Allied Force Headquarters in Algiers to soften the tone of propaganda to Italy so as to encourage the Italians to request surrender. It found support in this from Roosevelt, since these proposals were contrary to the unconditional surrender principle. At the end of May, the Allied Combined Chiefs of Staff responded to Eisenhower's request to take a less rigid stand:

> Most certainly we cannot tell the Italians that if they cease hostilities they will have a peace with honor. We cannot get away from unconditional surrender. All we can tell them is that they will be treated by us and the British with humanity and with the intention that the Italian people be reconstituted into a nation in accordance with the principles of self-determination. This latter should, of course, not include any form of fascism or dictatorship.[78]

Only on the eve of the landing, after a trial of strength between Eisenhower's command and the British government, was a compromise reached to make the propaganda more favorable to the Italians. The American propagandists, however, had repeatedly issued encouraging declarations that departed from the line agreed on and led to protests from the British.[79]

At the time of the landing, which was executed on the night of

July 9–10, Italy's departure from the war depended completely on its imminent military defeat. The reflections of this situation filtered up to the highest levels of the Allied governments. In the middle of July, Churchill, with obvious pleasure, informed Roosevelt of approaches from Italian commands in the Balkans and Greece and of German troop movements to reinforce the area. A few days later, Roosevelt confirmed that it appeared from American intelligence information that the Italians would not resist in case of an Allied attack, especially because their alternative was to be massacred by the Greeks and Slavs.[80]

Although marked by clashes and disagreements among the Allied commanders, the Sicilian operations turned out to be easier than anticipated and the feared Italian resistance did not materialize. On August 17, General Sir Harold Alexander informed Churchill of the end of the Sicilian campaign:

> Sicily invaded July 10. Messina entered August 16. Island taken in 38 days. Sicily has coastline 600 miles and area 10,000 square miles. Island is heavily fortified with concrete pill-boxes and wire. Axis garrison: Italian, 9 divisions; German, 4 divisions, equalling 13 divisions. Total forces: Italian, 315,000: German 90,000, making total 405,000 soldiers. Our forces: Seventh Army, 6 divisions, including airborne division; Eighth Army, 7 divisions, including airborne and armoured brigades, making Allied total 13 divisions. . . .
>
> It can be assumed that all Italian forces in island on July 10 have been destroyed, though a few battered units may have escaped to mainland. It is impossible yet to estimate booty and war material captured. Guns, tanks, rifles and machine-guns are lying scattered about all over island.[81]

Later that day Alexander wired, "At 10 this morning, August 17, the last German soldier fled from Sicily and the entire island is now in our hands."[82] Actually, in spite of this triumphant tone, the fact that the German troops had fully succeeded in withdrawing from the island was certainly not to be considered in a positive light, because the Allies would be facing at Salerno the same troops they had not been able to stop or capture in Sicily.

As soon as the success of the landing was clear, Churchill began to advocate continuing operations in the peninsula. He wrote Roosevelt on July 17, transmitting a message from South African Prime Minister Jan Smuts: "[C]ongratulations on the auspicious start of the Sicilian expedition. . . . [T]he question arises, what next? Should not the answer be Rome?" Churchill's plans were much more ambitious than he wanted them to appear. Two days later, on July 19, before any decision had been taken on continuing operations in Italy, Churchill wrote to General Alexander, encouraging him to use all his forces at the end of the battle for Sicily to reach Rome, from which a jump could be made to the Balkans. Alexander received the idea with enthusiasm. On July 22 he replied that Sicily was the jumping-off place for the advance toward Italy, but that it was essential to occupy the Balkan peninsula for control of the Mediterranean. He concluded, "We must unite the forces with our friends in the Balkans as soon as possible."[83]

There was strong opposition from the American Chiefs of Staff to any action in the Balkans. In addition, the attack on Sicily had been accepted by the American Joint Chiefs of Staff with the understanding that operations would stop there. However, Mussolini's fall on July 25 seemed to support the British theory that Italy was about to collapse. Urgent British requests to continue the campaign with a landing on the peninsula to push Italy out of the war were accepted when it became clear that the Allies were taking control of Sicily. The date and place of the landing – between September 9 and 11 at Salerno – were set at the Quebec Conference of 1943.[84] The plans for the landing at Salerno, code-named Avalanche, supported by a preliminary landing in Calabria, Operation Baytown, were therefore improvised; the troops used were less prepared than those which landed in Sicily, so that General Eisenhower, as commander of the Allied forces, feared up to the eve of the action that they would be pushed back into the sea. Thus he tried to capitalize on the success of the Sicilian landing, though he was aware of the risk implied in a frontal confrontation with the enemy forces on the mainland. For this reason, Eisenhower became the main advocate of an armistice with Italy after Mussolini fell. Italy's departure from the war would have eliminated some of the forces the Allies would have to face at Salerno and would have demoralized the remaining German troops.

6. The Landing in Sicily and the Crisis of the Italian Army

General Ambrosio appeared aware that the Italian armed forces would not be able to resist an Anglo-American attack on the peninsula after their severe defeats on all fronts. However, he continued for many months to delude himself into thinking that the attack would not come all that soon and that in the meantime Germany would concentrate its activities in the Mediterranean and come to Italy's aid, although he had been warning Mussolini against the precarious Italian military situation.[85] Ambrosio tried to put pressure on Mussolini to speak clearly to the Germans and confront them with the alternatives: either they must give priority to defending Italy and provide the necessary military aid, or Italy would be obliged to leave the alliance and ask for a separate peace. Mussolini maintained the illusion that he could persuade Hitler to make a separate peace with the Soviet Union, which would allow the Germans to concentrate their power in the Mediterranean. Hitler did not do this, but committed himself in the spring to another offensive on the Russian front. Given Mussolini's obvious reluctance to take a position independent of Germany, Ambrosio turned to the king with the same disappointing results, but he never thought of taking the initiative to approach the Anglo-Americans. The monarchy, Mussolini and the senior military leaders did nothing to set themselves loose from Germany, on which they were totally dependent up to the end and which they later blamed for the Italian catastrophe. Even Ambrosio's right-hand man, General Giuseppe Castellano, who appeared convinced from the beginning that Italy's military weakness left it no alternative but to break the alliance with the Germans and request a separate peace, was ready to change his position if Germany had been able to resume the offensive. In a memorandum to Ambrosio of May 21, 1943, Castellano concluded that defeat could be avoided and the war continued on Germany's side in case of a greater Anglo-American commitment to the war against Japan:

> The fact that the threat to Europe could disappear means that we should remain at our ally's side as in the past, since the differences in ideology and interests between the British and Americans on the conduct of the war can lead to a favorable situation for Germany. If Germany fares well in its battles this summer and has no other concerns from the Russian enemy, it could strike some hard blows. . . . [T]hen the Axis strategic situation changes completely and every "individual" move constitutes a false step. . . . [I]f the battle in the summer fails, the argument is the exact opposite.[86]

Not even the loss of Tunisia conveyed a sense of urgency to the Italian leaders, or convinced them that a landing was imminent and that the Italian preparations were insufficient to face it. Mussolini's "bagnasciuga" (shoreline) speech[87] was not only rhetoric. On June 18, 1943, Ambrosio too had maintained in a memorandum for Mussolini that the Allies could not allow themselves to be defeated because "the Americans would immediately leave Europe, concerned as they are with the Pacific," and "British public opinion and even more American public opinion are showing signs of impatience."[88]

Ambrosio did not seem particularly worried about a landing on the Italian islands or on the country's southern coast: "Aside from its doubtful chances of success, this attack would have only a local result and would not give the enemy an immediate gain of strategic importance that would have a profound impact on the final result of the conflict."[89]

Note that the fortified island of Pantelleria had fallen a week earlier, following Allied air raids, with a hasty and unjustifiable surrender that provoked the anger of the Germans engaged in its defense.[90]

The total lack of realism displayed in these incidents helps to explain the absurd manner and the delays that marked the Italian Supreme Command's decision to make contact with the Allies after Mussolini's fall and the ridiculous pretension of the Italian emissaries in lecturing the Anglo-Americans about their strategic interests in the Mediterranean.

The landing in Sicily was a rude awakening for everyone. The lack of realism was not confined to relations with the adversary, but affected the domestic front as well. Throughout Italy there were increasingly obvious signs that the regime had lost authority as a result of the widespread perception that Germany was bringing Italy to catastrophe and that its only hope was to leave the war. Everyone was aware that Italy was compelled to take the defensive, that it could soon be occupied and that its antiaircraft defenses could not prevent the massive air raids that were striking the large cities and industrial centers.

The effect of the raids on Italy's morale was devastating, because they convinced the population that their homes and workplaces could no longer be protected from enemy attack. The raids were more intense on the islands, where the scanty communications were seriously interrupted, food and clothing were scarce and the cost of living grew increasingly unsustainable.

Fascist propaganda had tried to reinforce the morale of the Sicilian population with bombastic phrases characterizing Sicily as "the strategic center of the Empire" or "the first line, the front of the 'fatherland,' " and assuring the people that in case of a landing every city in Sicily would be "a trench."[91] Aside from the rhetoric, the local authorities were concerned with the population's reaction to an invasion. According to the police chief of Agrigento, Sicily, "Most likely it will be passive, not because it is anti-patriotic, but because it was ignored when the food was distributed."[92] Asked about public reaction to one of Mussolini's speeches, the Carabinieri in Enna reported:

> The speech of the Duce has left the public indifferent. . . . The speech . . . was not listened to by a majority of the citizens, because they have no longer any faith in him who guides the destinies of the nation. . . .
> The public, besides the things of primary necessity, needs soap – which now has been turned over completely to the Armed Forces –

oil, sugar (which are not distributed), clothing, and shoes that have completely disappeared from the market.

To all this must be added the continuous bombings of the large and small towns of the Island, without sufficient opposition from our side, which has lowered the morale of the people to a point that they pray for the end of the war as a holy liberation.[93]

This report is dated July 9, the day before the landing and with it the "holy liberation." In some sectors, the Sicilian bulwark collapsed in a few days. In others, there was greater resistance, especially in those areas the Germans had reinforced. But the entire island was conquered in little more than a month. The landing in Sicily made plain the inadequacy of the Axis forces – there were two German divisions in Sicily – and the lack of Italian military preparation. The operation was executed with total control of the sea and overwhelming Allied air superiority. The operation of the scant Axis air forces was reduced by the Anglo-Americans' systematic destruction of the island's air bases. The clear disproportion between the forces was the main reason for the Italian army's disintegration. However, the scale of the phenomenon requires further explanation. The Italian troops were disoriented from the start. On July 16, General Alfredo Guzzoni, commander of the armed forces in Sicily, denounced

the shameful phenomenon of disintegration that has afflicted some units and services of all the armed forces located in Sicily – with no exceptions – which casts deep discredit on the Italian soldier, especially in comparison with the Allied armed forces.[94]

The commanders accused the troops of lacking "moral fiber," while at the same time they themselves were covering up or minimizing very serious episodes, such as the one at the piazza of Augusta, which was abandoned by the field army before it was attacked and where war material and even the code books were left intact.[95] Colonel Schmaltz, the commander of a German detachment situated near Augusta, replied as follows to an explanation by Ambrosio that the Italian units were subjected to intense air raids:

General Ambrosio's note does not report the facts correctly. I would not know how to justify the behavior of the soldiers at Augusta. I never saw these alleged air raids. There was no will to oppose the enemy landing. However, the courage of the units that did resist is worthy of note. . . . [T]he lack of fighting spirit among the Italians in Sicily came from the fact that the will to fight originates with commanders and these commanders had lost control of the situation. . . . I who am familiar with the entire unpleasant reality am nauseated by the diplomatic and ironic style of Ambrosio's note.[96]

The lack of confidence and the feeling that the struggle was in vain were reinforced by the Allies' effective propaganda, which promised to let the Sicilian soldiers who surrendered go free and not to consider them prisoners of war. These feelings were fueled by contact with the civilian population, tired by continuous air raids and convinced that a strenuous resistance would only cause the destruction of the island. Further, some of the troops were Sicilians, and this encouraged desertion by those who decided to return to their families. In addition to the many soldiers who abandoned their posts to return home, entire units disintegrated and ferry boats were abandoned by their crews. To make the situation still more confusing, moving in the opposite direction of the soldiers and civilians who wanted to leave the island were false volunteers, "Sicilian soldiers from every part of the peninsula," who with the excuse of going to defend Sicily were trying to return home.

On July 27 Mario Roatta, chief of staff of the army, described the situation in a letter to the commanding generals of the field armies. He expressed the fear that widespread desertion and demoralization might extend to the troops in the rest of the peninsula and the occupied territories:

During the operations in Sicily the population occupied the communication links in a disorderly manner, blocking them in spite of orders to the contrary.

- Groups of people, in spite of posted guards, have demolished a pier, thinking that it could attract enemy naval gunfire.
- Soldiers at antiaircraft batteries, Milamart batteries, airfields, supply depots, etc. have abandoned their posts, fleeing in dis-

order, often in cars or other vehicles, by train or road, toward the Strait of Messina.

- Other units, although compact and orderly, have moved on their own, removing batteries that were still useful from their positions.
- Deserting soldiers from Sicilian provinces have gone home, sometimes wearing civilian clothes; . . .
- At the same time, Sicilian soldiers have come from all parts of the peninsula to Villa San Giovanni and Messina and once they reached the island they continued towards their families' homes rather than fight. And some groups of these "volunteers" made scenes when they were stopped by units assigned to police duties, in the peninsula and Sicily.
- Serious disorder has arisen, a sorry sight having bad effects on the troops as a whole, and a notable obstacle to reinforcement operations, so much so that once at Messina it was even impossible for reinforcements to land and proceed.

It was only with forceful reaction, by executing several individuals, including some officers, that it was possible to reestablish order across the Strait.[97]

Desertions reached very high levels in the "Assietta" division: at the beginning of August 9,110 soldiers had disappeared or deserted – nearly the whole division. In the "Aosta" division, in the same period, 51 officers and 2,635 noncommissioned officers and soldiers were reported absent.[98]

Most of the population lined up with the "liberators" at the moment of the landing, and there were even episodes of sabotage by both civilians and the military.

Official sources almost never mention the truly miserable hygienic conditions or the state of the units' clothing and rations. There were many cases of typhus, and scabies was widespread. Clothing was often dirty and torn, and shoes were in short supply.

In this confused and uncertain situation there were frequent incidents between German soldiers and the Italian civilian population and military. The presence of German soldiers on the island from 1941 on had led to complaints from the population, mostly because of the Germans' behavior toward Sicilian women, but tension broke out during the island's defense, especially because of Italian desertions and the difficult military situation. In many cases the Germans tried to assume command, taking advantage of the fact that they possessed antitank and antiaircraft weapons the Italians did not have. However, the most frequent episodes involved the Germans' confiscation of vehicles from the Italian military at gunpoint during the retreat, sometimes giving rise to violent confrontations.[99]

German soldiers often seized peasants' animals, including donkeys, mules and horses, which were vital to the victims in that time of wartime poverty.[100] Violent clashes sometimes followed, as recounted by the Sicilian writer Leonardo Sciascia:

> A man from Cesarò was riding a mule along country road during the days when the Germans were holding the front at Troina, with a fine machine gun attached to the saddle.
>
> He ran into a man from another town and the machine gun caught the other man's eye.
>
> "Where did you get it?" the other man asked.
> "If you want, there's another one," the Cesarò man answered.
> "A gun like that? Where? And how did you get hold of it?"
> "I was riding my mule," said the Cesarò man. And he stopped, as if he wanted to conclude the conversation.
> "You were riding your mule, yes . . . And what happened then?"
> "It happened that there were two Germans."
> "And what about the two Germans?"
> "They wanted my mule."
> "And then?"
> "I don't have anything but my mule, but I had my axe with me."
> "Your axe?"
> "My axe . . . There were two of them. They wanted to take my mule."
> "I understand . . . And what did you do?"
> "I have just this mule. If they take it away from me I'm dead. But I had my axe with me."
> "And then?"
> "I hit one of them with it and I cut the other one open."

An attempted requisition or a raid led to an uprising against the Germans in Mascalucia, another town near Mount Etna. The

Germans killed a man in their attempt, but unfortunately he was the uncle of a man with a weapons shop and he handed out weapons to the population.

The first resistance to the Germans as well as the first German atrocity on Italian territory was in the area around Mount Etna, while the Germans were still allies, although Mussolini had already fallen.[101]

The events in Sicily in the weeks following the landing, vividly described by Sciascia, presage Italy's future experience, from the disintegration of the army to the beginnings of the Resistance.

CHAPTER TWO

From July 25 to September 8, 1943

1. The Fall of Mussolini

The fall of Mussolini on July 25 resulted from two successive events, both of which originated within the regime: the no-confidence vote of the Fascist Grand Council, the party's highest organ, and the decision of King Victor Emmanuel III to request Mussolini's resignation. Mussolini had probably agreed to summon the Grand Council on July 24 (the Council had not met since 1939) in order to face the internal opposition and reduce it to minority status. However, after a heated discussion lasting for several hours, the motion presented by Dino Grandi requesting that the king resume his constitutional powers was put to a vote and approved 19 to 7. The following day, July 25, the king finally took the initiative, not only of replacing Mussolini with Field Marshal Pietro Badoglio, but also of having him arrested. This took the Duce completely by surprise, as he had been convinced he could count on the king's support. In a few hours a regime that had lasted twenty years was brought to an end. The anti-Fascist opposition had nothing to do with Mussolini's overthrow. In the preceding weeks, the king had limited himself to receiving a few pre-Fascist figures, such as Ivanoe Bonomi and Vittorio Emanuele Orlando, who had asked him to take the initiative.

Some anti-Fascist parties, such as the Communist Party, the Action Party and the Christian Democratic Party (the new name assumed by the old Catholic party, the Partito Popolare Italiano), had begun to reorganize and proselytize in 1942, but Mussolini's resignation caught them by surprise as well.

The common goal of those voting against Mussolini on the Council was to sacrifice him in order to maintain the regime he had created and to preserve the monarchy. According to Grandi, the July 25 events were not meant to put an end to Fascism or to lead to Mussolini's arrest. Grandi was thinking of a government that would join Fascists and moderate anti-Fascists to support the monarchy, but without repudiating the past.[1] King Victor Emmanuel intended to retain an authoritarian regime, and never even considered seeking support from the anti-Fascist forces. As head of the government, a military officer like Badoglio would maintain control of the country and the army for an initial period, which was probably regarded as transitory, with the government later being entrusted to Grandi; the king even suggested to the Allies that Grandi, whom he referred to as a "symbol of anti-Fascism," be appointed minister of foreign affairs, but Eisenhower firmly rejected the idea. In the end the replacement of Mussolini by Badoglio – that is, a "constitutional" crisis within the Fascist regime – was presented as a military coup to bring Fascism down.[2]

As soon as Badoglio took office, he hastened to proclaim to the nation the decision of his government to continue the war as an ally of Germany. His phrase "The war will go on," however, looked like a ruse to gain time and to organize an armistice with the British and American governments.

The days from July 25 to September 8 are among the most confused and dramatic in Italy's history. They are known as "the forty-five days." Among Badoglio's first moves was to get rid of the most conspicuous symbols of the old regime. The Fascist Party, the Special Court for the Defense of the State, which had tried the regime's political opponents, and the Grand Council of Fascism were all dissolved. Badoglio also nominated a cabinet, most of whose members, however, were representatives of the old ruling or military elite. The only concession to the opposition was the appointment of some anti-Fascists to the Council of Corporations.

The situation required immediate action and a plan for withdrawing from the war. The new government found itself faced with three options: (1) announce the end of the alliance with Germany and immediately place itself on the side of the Anglo-Americans; (2) continue the alliance with Germany, but attempt to convince the Germans not to oppose a separate peace between Italy and the Anglo-Americans; or (3) pretend to want to continue the war on Germany's side, while at the same time initiating surrender negotiations with the Anglo-Americans. The first option was rejected immediately. It had been proposed by Dino Grandi,[3] who had offered to go at once to Lisbon and Madrid to contact the Allies. The king feared such a move because it would lead to a direct clash with the Germans without having the support of the Anglo-Americans, and because it would mean a total break with a past that the king and Badoglio not only had participated in but also were jointly responsible for. However, no one made a choice between the other two possibilities; instead, an attempt was made to pursue both simultaneously. There were hopes of persuading the Germans to accept Italy's withdrawal from the war in exchange for Italy's neutrality and the gradual transfer of Italy's control of the Balkan and Greek fronts to the Reich's armed forces. When it became clear that Germany was not disposed to do this, Badoglio contacted the Allies.

The hope of persuading Germany to accept Italy's departure from the war was shown to be baseless because, as we will see, Hitler had no intention of losing Italy and meant to make the king and the new government pay for their "betrayal." With hindsight it seems contradictory of the government and the king to have considered such a solution when, at the same time, there were fears of a German coup supported by the Fascists. Paolo Puntoni wrote in his diary on July 29:

> . . . the situation is getting more serious. Some senior fascist representatives who cannot be located apparently have been able to contact the Germans in order to organize an armed revolt.[4]

General Ambrosio wrote in his diary at that time: "Hitler feels even more closely tied to Mussolini. It will be even harder to get free of the Germans." A little later, he returned to the topic: ". . . a meeting in which we tell them we cannot go on with the war would be followed by immediate action."[5]

From July 25 to September 8, 1943

In the days following July 25 the situation became more complicated. On the domestic front, the feared Fascist reaction to Mussolini's fall did not materialize and the party seemed to disappear into a void. However, there was an immediate outburst of joy among the Italians, who interpreted the dismissal of Mussolini as the prelude to Italy's imminent departure from the war. The first spontaneous manifestations in favor of peace and the monarchy were followed by the first political requests and a series of strikes and agitation. The government and the military authorities, concerned that a revolutionary movement might arise, acted immediately. General Mario Roatta, chief of the Army General Staff, issued a directive on July 26 to repress any manifestations that could disturb public order, commanding the units to proceed "in combat formation" and always shoot "to kill." The "leaders and instigators of disorder" and "military personnel engaged in duties of public order who make the least gesture of solidarity with disturbers of public order either are in rebellion or are disobeying orders" and must be shot immediately. To justify the severity of these measures, Roatta's circular declared summarily that "a little bloodshed at the beginning will save rivers of blood later." The order was carried out in Bari against demonstrators demanding the liberation of political prisoners and an end to the war. Seventeen were killed and many more wounded, some being very young. There were incidents throughout Italy.[6]

The severity with which the popular uprisings were repressed can be explained only by the fear of the Italian military leadership that it could not maintain control of the domestic situation and its assumption that an extended Communist organization was prepared to throw the country into chaos. Evidence of this is the exclusion of Communists and anarchists from the political prisoners being freed and the many circulars prohibiting military personnel from joining political parties and warning against the danger of Communist infiltration into the army.[7] Roatta and Antonio Sorice, the minister of war, driven by what was taking place in Sicily, sent a series of circulars to corps commanders asking them for "efforts to motivate the soldiers," to convince them that the war would have to go on and to urge them on to energetic and disciplined action. Sorice affirmed this in a circular of August 1, 1943, which was transmitted the following week to several command levels:

> To pronounce the word "peace" in the present situation, when our people's moral and spiritual force is not only intact but has gained proud and renewed vigor from the recent domestic events, is the same as giving the enemy a strong offensive weapon that can be used for blackmail, and not understanding our soldiers' capacity to resist. Faithful to the glorious warlike traditions of the race, they do their duty courageously on the field of battle.[8]

2. Hitler's Plans for a Coup in Italy and Italian Countermeasures

Mussolini's fall on July 25 confirmed the fears Hitler had repeatedly expressed in previous months of an Italian surrender and a separate peace with the Allies.[9] The Germans had long since taken over strategic direction of the war in the Mediterranean and had shown that they had Germany's interests alone at heart. From the spring of 1943 on, Hitler had decided that "if necessary, German troops would control Italian positions and defend them," even at the price of completely deposing the Italian commands.[10] Starting in May, after the Allied conquest of Tunisia, the German High Command began to make plans for directly assuming the defense of Italy and the Balkans in case of a collapse, or an armistice with the Anglo-Americans, in order to be ready even for an armed conflict with their Italian allies.[11] Italy's military weakness, its insufficient and obsolete weaponry and the demoralization of its troops made prolonged Italian resistance unlikely in case of an Allied landing, even if a decision were made to carry on with the war to the bitter end. On the other hand, the Germans could not permit the loss of Italy, with its industrial and agricultural resources of the Po Valley; also, if it were lost, the Anglo-Americans would be in contact with Germany's southern border. On Hitler's request, Field Marshal Erwin Rommel drew up a plan for defending and occupying Italy in the event of its defection and in July concluded that "we cannot hold the entire peninsula without the Italian Army."[12] It was therefore appropriate to push for a withdrawal from southern Italy and a defense only from the Apennines.

Hitler's reaction to the news of Mussolini's dismissal was violent. Convinced of "Italian treachery" and believing that the new government meant to surrender, Hitler thought at first of arranging a coup, with the arrest of Badoglio and the king and the restoration of a Fascist regime in Berlin under Farinacci, pending "taking possession of Mussolini."[13] He later decided to take a more cautious line, pretending to believe Badoglio's professions of loyalty, but only to gain time and prepare to occupy at least northern Italy.

Goebbels and other German leaders were also aware that, with Mussolini's fall, "the prestige of the authoritarian form of government" had been "shaken to an extent that still cannot be estimated."[14] They feared that Italy's example could lead to hopes for an imminent end to the war in Germany as well, weakening German resistance, and could be followed by the capitulation of Hungary and other satellite states. This, in fact, was the effect the news of Mussolini's deposition had on the populations of Axis countries.[15] Something had to be done right away. A few days before the fall of Mussolini, on July 19 at a meeting in Feltre, the Germans had bluntly refused to send reinforcements to Italy on the grounds that no more divisions were available. However, the situation changed radically with the news that the Duce had resigned. The first concern was to safeguard the Balkans, where the Germans thought the Anglo-Americans would probably land. Immediately after Mussolini's "resignation" on July 26, Hitler issued a directive that the Italian occupation forces in the Dodecanese Islands be put under German command and that Italian units in control of crucial positions be "reinforced" with German contingents.[16] The Italian troops placed under German command and their relations with the German forces would make it more difficult for the Italians to free themselves from German control when the armistice was proclaimed.

At the same time, approximately eight divisions poured into Italy, doubling in a few days the number of German troops in the peninsula, in sharp contrast to the declarations made at Feltre that there were not enough German forces available to defend Italy. They "acted like occupation troops in an enemy country,"[17] taking control of the main lines of communication and the railroad around the Brenner Pass, a critical artery for Germany. They set up checkpoints at frontiers and power plants without asking permission or offering explanations to the Italian Supreme Command. The German purpose was very clear: predicting that Italy would leave the alliance and that the Allies would land on the peninsula, they perceived their greatest danger to be the isolation of their troops to the south. The Germans therefore wished to assume control of the most important part of Italy, the north, and abandon the south, where no further troops were sent. The units pouring into the Alto Adige region, this formerly-Austrian territory, declared openly that they wanted to retake what Germans and Austrians called South Tyrol. There were several cases of abuse and violence against soldiers and civilians.[18] The Italian Supreme Command protested, but obtained only delayed excuses. Roatta explained the impasse of the Badoglio government:

> Our military situation generally and throughout the peninsula, with the latter being complicated by the problems of public order referred to above, does not permit us to oppose the German measures with force.
>
> On the other hand, even if material circumstances had allowed us an effective armed action, it most likely would not have been carried out because we were not then oriented to a conflict with Germany, or even a simple separation from her.
>
> The measures taken by the General Staff, on orders from the Supreme Command, to face this developing situation were not those of open opposition, but rather were precautionary and in harmony, within the limits of the possible, with the need then considered pre-eminent of defending ourselves against the Anglo-Americans.[19]

In other words, according to Roatta, the Italian authorities still intended to continue the war and follow a prudent line so as not to provoke the Germans. Pietro Acquarone, minister of the Royal Household, issued a similar statement to the commission chaired by

From July 25 to September 8, 1943

Mario Palermo, according to his testimony, in response to the request to explain why

> at the time of Mussolini's arrest no plan was prepared to disengage Italy from Germany. Acquarone answered: "no one posed the problem of ending the war on Germany's side on July 25, 1943. We were all concerned to free Italy from Mussolini, which seemed to be a very difficult problem to solve.[20]

The German High Command lost no time. On August 1 it set in motion a plan to occupy Italy. The code name of the operation was *Achse* (Axis), a new version of the previous plan *Alaric*; it would replace Badoglio with a Fascist government, disarm units of the Italian army north of Rome and withdraw German troops from the south to prevent them from becoming isolated and attacked from the rear by an enemy landing. The German intentions became clear during an episode in Greece in which an erroneous interpretation of an order led to the surrounding and disarming of some Italian units, almost in anticipation of what would take place on September 8.

The tension between the two countries and German mistrust of Italy were emphasized in two meetings held in August to define a common strategy in light of a new Allied offensive: the first on August 6 at Tarvisio and the second on the 15th at Bologna. At Tarvisio, von Ribbentrop aggressively asked Italian Foreign Minister Raffaele Guariglia if there had not been "direct negotiations with British or American elements."[21] Ambrosio, for his part, protested the decision to send German divisions into Italy without informing the Supreme Command so that

> he now feels that he is no longer master in his own house. . . . The German divisions, which entered Italy with no previous agreement, and in some cases with unjustifiable aggressive action, are assuming positions that no longer appear to respond to the interests of common defense, but only to the interests of Germany.[22]

Since these German moves openly violated Italian sovereignty, the tone of Ambrosio's protests was all too moderate. The Germans minimized Ambrosio's accusations concerning the behavior of their troops, who looked on Italy as an "occupied country" rather than as an ally. It was already clear at Tarvisio that the Germans did not intend to give explanations for the movements of their units in Italy; on the other hand, they were irritated by the Italian request to withdraw their Fourth Army from France and reduce its forces in the Balkans, and maintained that the question would have to be submitted to Hitler. Germany's policy was definitive by now: to reinforce its control of northern Italy with its own troops and leave the defense of southern Italy to the Italians, in order to avoid the exposure of its army to an attack from two directions. It was after the Tarvisio Conference that Ambrosio decided to send General Giuseppe Castellano on a mission to the Allies. The increased hostility shown by the Germans during the Bologna meeting would finally convince Roatta that the Germans meant to attack. Thus the German decision to execute a coup in Italy preceded the Italian decision to surrender. If that is not enough to prove that there was a "German betrayal," it can certainly be maintained, as Roatta wrote, that "German aggression came first."[23]

After July 25, Marshal Albert Kesselring, German commander in chief in Italy, lost the confidence of Hitler, who regarded the marshal as pro-Italian. He kept secret from Kesselring his plans for overthrowing the Badoglio government and entrusted to Rommel the command of the German army in northern Italy. Kesselring in fact opposed the use of force and was inclined to trust the new government.[24] In contrast to the attitude of the German High Command and Hitler, who gave priority to the defense of northern Italy and to relinquishing the defense of southern Italy, Kesselring supported the Italian request to move a portion of the divisions entering Italy to the south, but the answer was negative. In the second half of August, the German High Command confirmed to Kesselring orders to arrange a retreat in central Italy and take steps to deal with an Italian defection in case of an Anglo-American landing.[25]

The possibility of a coup organized by the Germans to bring Mussolini back to power became the most immediate danger for the Badoglio government. Even if the commander of the Fascist militia was replaced and the militia absorbed by the army, it was soon clear that there were close ties between Fascist elements and German agents who had come to Rome. In the following weeks, the fear of a coup was reflected in information from the intelligence services on suspected movements and contacts between Fascist groups and Germans and the increasingly aggressive attitude of the latter.[26] There was also the unknown element of the behavior of the Italian Military Intelligence Service (SIM). According to Ambrosio, this service "was closely connected with the analogous German office and its members had friendly contacts with their German colleagues,"[27] to such an extent as to make it impossible to use the SIM's information network. General Cesare Amé, head of the SIM, was on friendly terms with Admiral Canaris, the famous head of the German intelligence service, later implicated in the July 1944 attempted coup against Hitler, who showed himself willing to collaborate in the new situation.[28] It is not clear why the competent Amè, with his precious connection, was replaced by General Giacomo Carboni, who was put in charge of the SIM even though he was already in command of the motorized corps that was to defend Rome. He proved completely inadequate at both jobs.[29] He did nothing to neutralize a possible coup by the Germans. It would have been difficult for anyone to take the situation in hand in a few weeks, but Carboni demonstrated a degree of superficiality and incompetence equaled by none.

Fear of a punitive reaction by the German armed forces conditioned every move by the government. A paradoxical situation developed: Badoglio delayed contacting the Anglo-Americans for fear of making the Germans suspicious, while the Germans were convinced that armistice negotiations were already under way and tried to find evidence of "Italian betrayal" ready to come out in the open.

The Badoglio government could not make a decision, in spite of public pressure to take Italy out of the war and the heavy Anglo-American bombardment of Italian cities. There was no way out for Italy – pushed by an ally preparing to act as an enemy, pouring its divisions in to occupy strategic positions, and enemies preparing to land on the peninsula, refusing all negotiations in advance. There was no room for an agreement with either, but Badoglio and the king did not realize this and showed themselves totally incapable of facing the situation, dragging Italy by their inaction into the greatest military disaster in its history. Concerned more with their own fate than with that of Italy, they relegated to second place the necessary preparations for the moment the armistice was announced. Their only concern was to maintain secrecy to avoid giving the Germans a pretext for a coup. Thus the king and Badoglio issued no directives to the Supreme Command and the Army General Staff to "orient" their various subordinate commands to the possibility of an armistice with the Anglo-Americans for fear the Germans would get wind of it.

For the entire first half of August, the Italian Supreme Command directed its attention to continuing the war on Germany's side while awaiting an armistice.[30] At the same time, the Italians adopted a series of measures to confront and invalidate a probable German attack. As General Roatta wrote in a report in early 1944 on the events of those days, none of the measures taken during "the forty-five days" between the fall of Mussolini and the announcement of the armistice even considered the possibility of an armistice with the Anglo-Americans. Instead, they were aimed at "avoiding a possible German coup" intended to replace the Badoglio government with a Fascist one.[31]

The Army General Staff prepared two documents: the order "111 CT" was sent to all commanders between August 10 and 15. Toward the end of August, at Ambrosio's request, the Staff prepared "Memoria 44," which was an expansion of the document "111 CT" and which was also transmitted, between September 2 and 4 exclusively, to commanders directly subordinate to the Army General Staff, that is, to forces stationed in Italy. Both documents were truly defensive regarding a possible German attack and made no reference of any kind to a possible armistice. The words "German attack" were not used in the text, to avoid provoking the Germans if the documents became known to them, but there were references to "non-national" or "Communist" forces, which would act "in agreement or not with the Fascists." For the same reason, these measures were transmitted to officers with orders to destroy the documents after reading them. There are therefore now neither originals nor copies but only transcriptions made later.[32] Orders were given to react to German violence "only if provoked," to defend installations, to monitor German troop movements and to arrange surprise attacks against vital elements of their armed forces, such as vehicle parks, munitions and fuel dumps and airports.

Memoria 44 repeated the guidance already given but also provided other instructions, including the interruption, "at whatever cost, even with full-scale attacks on the guard forces, of the railroads and the main alpine highways," and set specific tasks for each division. The division in Sardinia was instructed to "first eliminate the German troops present on the island, then prepare for further missions."

These directives were to be carried out on the orders of the Supreme Command or, if communications were cut off, at the initiative of the commanders whenever the Germans "resorted to collective hostilities that could not be confused with isolated incidents."[33]

Two alpine divisions were then sent to the Alto Adige to protect that region and the garrison at the port of La Spezia was reinforced where a large portion of the fleet was located. Only after the Bologna meeting did the Supreme Command give permission to withdraw some of the troops from the Balkans. However, this withdrawal had hardly gotten under way when the armistice was announced.

While these anti-German plans were under way, military collaboration with Germany regarding the imminent Anglo-American landing continued. The attitude of senior military officers emerged clearly from the proceedings of the Palermo Commission. Roatta's testimony was of special interest, since he admitted that Ambrosio had discussed the possibility of an armistice some days before his departure for the August 15 meeting at Bologna between the representatives of the German and Italian General Staffs, where a decision had to be made about the deployment of troops in defense of the peninsula.[34] During that interrogation, Roatta justified the Italian refusal in Bologna of the German proposal to move Italian troops to the south-central portion of the peninsula and the

Germans to the north with the highly unusual proposition that he did not want to "let our game become known," because if he accepted, the Germans would have had evidence that the Italians did not intend "to defend Italy jointly."[35] In doing this, Roatta lost a unique opportunity to concentrate Italian troops in south-central Italy and liberate at least that region from the Germans. However, he did more: at that same meeting he requested and obtained a German division to reinforce Sardinia, the possession of which was of fundamental strategic importance for Italy.[36] It might be thought that Roatta acted as he did because he was pro-German, but neither Badoglio nor Ambrosio acted differently. Badoglio rejected Ambrosio's proposal of approximately August 20 to begin to "brief the peripheral commands," especially in the Balkans, stating, according to Ambrosio's testimony, that he would have preferred the loss of even half a million men "rather than suffer the far more serious consequences of an immediate German reaction provoked by information leaks."[37] For his part, Ambrosio proceeded to act as if he anticipated a continuation of the German alliance, continuing to request more German troops in Italy, perhaps to avoid making the Germans suspicious or perhaps to keep a foot in both camps.

There was no change in Italian policy that was not provoked by German moves. In collaboration with the German command, the Italian Supreme Command continued throughout August and until the armistice was announced to arrange defensive measures against an Anglo-American landing. Early in September directives were sent to all commanders exhorting them to collaborate completely with the Germans and warning them to prepare for any enemy landings. Security considerations cannot justify the order the Supreme Command sent early in September to Headquarters Army Group East to ask German assistance to defend the ports of Durrës in Albania and Kotor in Yugoslavia, in view of an eventual Anglo-American landing. It was Durrës from which, according to Memoria 44, the divisions of the Ninth Army were to embark to reach safety.[38]

It was only on September 5 that Ambrosio decided to draw up Promemoria no. 1, which included instructions analogous to those in Memoria 44, to the General Staffs of the army, navy and air force, and issued on the 6th. Promemoria no. 2, addressed to the forces directly subordinate to the Supreme Command (Herzegovina, Montenegro, Albania, Greece including Crete, and the Dodecanese Islands), was directed to the headquarters of Army Group East, the headquarters of the Eleventh Army and the headquarters of the armed forces in the Dodecanese Islands.

In drawing up the orders, it occurred to General Rossi that he could not use Memoria 44 alone as a model, since Italy's commitments made in the armistice had to be kept in mind.[39] Thus, in Promemoria no. 1, which continued to consider only the "case in which German forces independently undertake armed hostile acts against Italian government organizations and armed forces," there appeared the order to prevent British prisoners from falling into German hands, with a distinction, however, between white and black prisoners.[40]

Promemoria no. 2 opened with the sentence "Special circumstances regarding public order can prevent our surrendering our weapons independently of the Germans." It went on to issue a series of instructions, among them to "guarantee the possession of the main ports in the worst of cases, especially Kotor and Durrës." As for the Dodecanese Islands, "the Commander in Chief is authorized to pursue such policy with respect to the Germans as he deems appropriate." However, it was added that "when it can be anticipated that the Germans will use force, immediate steps should be taken to disarm German units in the Archipelago."[41] This warning was never to reach its addressees, since for the most part it was preferable to summon the senior commanders to Rome. They were therefore surprised by the announcement of the armistice.

3. The Anglo-American Governments' Reaction to July 25 and the Start of the Armistice Negotiations

It is difficult to disentangle the series of misunderstandings, deceptions and illusions that marked the negotiations between Italy and the Anglo-Americans after Mussolini's fall without clarifying the mistaken assumptions on which they were based and the erroneous assessments of the situation by both sides.

First, the perception of an immense Allied military force strongly influenced the choices made by the Italian government. Not knowing, obviously, that the Allies' main objective was northern France, the Italian military and political leaders thought that a major landing on the peninsula or in the Balkans was imminent. This overestimation of Anglo-American power was due partly to the success of Allied propaganda, which for months had been proclaiming its own superiority and invincibility, and partly to the effects of the continuous bombing raids on Italian cities, and was confirmed by the quantity of Allied forces employed in the landing in Sicily. If such a deployment of forces had been used for this rather limited operation, could smaller forces be used for a landing on the peninsula, defended as it was by more numerous Italian and German forces?

Second, the Italian military leadership was convinced that, if the main objective of the landing was the occupation of Italy, it would take place north of Rome, because a landing to the south would exclude a rapid advance by the Anglo-American forces.

Finally, the Italians unjustifiably overestimated their own negotiating strength. The idea cultivated by Fascism that Italy had become a "great power" did not disappear, and the Italian government deluded itself into thinking that the Allies, in order to eliminate Italy from the conflict, would not insist on unconditional surrender if the new government conveyed an "anti-Fascist" image.[42] Here too the illusion was fueled by Allied propaganda and the statements by the most senior Allied leaders. To persuade the Italians to capitulate while at the same time requiring unconditional surrender, the Allied propagandists attempted to show that there was "nothing dishonorable" in the idea of unconditional surrender, and used that expression as little as possible, substituting for it the term "honorable capitulation."[43] The ambiguity of this expression was stressed by Harold Macmillan, then British resident minister at Allied headquarters, when he noted ironically:

I think the definition must be that the capitulation is Italian and the honourable part of it is British. In other words there is no conflict between Honourable Capitulation and Unconditional Surrender. What it means is that it is our duty to see that these conditions which are to be signed without argument do not in fact impose any dishonourable obligations upon the Italians.[44]

In May 1943, the Voice of America warned of an intensifation of the air raids if Italy did not accept withdrawal "with honor" in order to achieve a just peace.[45] In a joint declaration of July 16, Churchill and Roosevelt stated that "the sole hope for Italy [lay] in honourable capitulation." The reference to "honourable" conditions was later taken up by Eisenhower in a message to the Italians transmitted on July 29, after the fall of Mussolini.[46] These statements led the Italian side to hope for a negotiated peace with moderate conditions and to give little weight to the principle of unconditional surrender. A recurring theme in the Italian approach was that it would be in the Allies' interest to avoid a German occupation of Italy and the danger of a revolution there. The Italian government was convinced that the Anglo-Americans would prefer a neutral Italy to a German occupation and the imposition of a new Fascist government. As previously noted, this was just the solution the Foreign Office preferred, since Italy would then be a burden on German resources.

Although the Allies had been discussing the possibility of Italy's collapse for months, Mussolini's fall on July 25 found them completely unprepared for the new situation. Neither Roosevelt nor Churchill expected Mussolini to give up power so easily, and the two Allied commands were not ready to dictate surrender terms when requested to do so by the Italians.

Mussolini's fall was regarded by the British and American governments as confirmation of the collapse of the Fascist regime, soon to be followed by a request for an armistice from the new Italian government. It led to sudden euphoria in governing circles in Washington and London. The military and political consequences of Mussolini's ouster and what policy to adopt toward the new government were the objects of an intense exchange of telegrams between Roosevelt and Churchill from July 26 to 30, 1943. The two leaders were convinced that the Italian government would stay in control of the country and that the Germans would withdraw from the Balkans as well as from Italy, even after some encounters with the Italian army. In "Thoughts on the Fall of Mussolini," a July 26 memorandum to the British government, with a copy to Roosevelt, Churchill anticipated an ideal scenario: the surrender of Italian forces in Italy, the Balkans and Greece to the Allies after these forces had driven the Germans out of Italy. In a transmittal letter Churchill explained his position on the Badoglio government: "I do not think myself that we should be too particular in dealing with any Non-Fascist Government, even if it is not all we should like. Now Mussolini is gone, I would deal with any Non Fascist Italian Government which can deliver the goods."[47]

Roosevelt fully shared Churchill's optimism on possible developments in the Italian situation, his confidence that the Germans would withdraw and his assessment of the need to deal with "any person or persons in Italy who can best give us first disarmament and second assurance against chaos," even if "some contentious people" were getting ready "to make a row if we seem to recognize the House of Savoy or Badoglio."[48] It appears they were victims of their own propaganda, according to which the population and the army in Italy were ready and willing to drive out "the German intruders,"[49] who had caused so much destruction and misery in Italy. Obviously their judgment was influenced by the situation before July 25, when there were only a few German divisions there. They therefore underestimated the German capacity to take control. Further, they did not consider the presence among senior Italian army officers of pro-Germans or at least those who favored continuing the war on Germany's side.

It is difficult to reconstruct the attitude of the Italian military leaders concerning this situation. After the war, they all insisted they were anti-German. One of the numerous memoranda prepared for the Office of Strategic Services (OSS) by General Carboni – which, like all Carboni's writings, must be carefully verified – describes the situation as follows:

In military circles, the most senior officers were divided into two camps. There was a minority motivated mostly by the desire to keep the ranks and positions they had attained. This group would have wanted the intensification of the war on the German side, adapting to an interference in the command structure that was even more thorough and obvious than what was already in place. There were more of these officers in the navy and air force than in the army. Most senior officers, however, favored immediate negotiations with the Anglo-Americans for a prompt departure from the war and a cancellation of the alliance with Germany. Within this majority, some believed that Italy was exhausted and could not sustain any more war effort. Others thought that Italy should take up arms against Germany on the Allied side in order to make up for the negative military efforts of the past few years, due not to a lack of courage or military capacity, but to the lack of enthusiasm for a war forced upon Italy.[50]

In the month following Mussolini's fall, Western Allied leaders maintained quite an optimistic stance on the Italian situation despite the growing presence of the German troops in Italy and persisting pro-German feelings among Italian military commanders. Thus, the Foreign Office in mid-August was still arguing that the prospect of a German occupation of Italy, on which the Badoglio government was insisting, was "nonsense."[51]

Further, the position taken by Roosevelt contradicted the principle of unconditional surrender. After maintaining for months with the British government and the U.S. military that there could be no negotiations with any government before such a surrender, Roosevelt was quite willing now to deal with Badoglio, even if the official American government position was much more intransigent. In a broadcast statement of July 28, Roosevelt himself reemphasized the principle of unconditional surrender.

The directives issued by the Office of War Information (OWI) for radio transmission to Europe left no room for doubt: "America's aim in this war is to destroy fascism, and whether Badoglio, Mussolini or others like them are the rulers does not matter."[52] The directive recorded Badoglio's role in the World War I disaster at Caporetto, his approval of Graziani's atrocities in Libya, his participation in the Ethiopian campaign and his willingness to receive favors from the Nazis. On July 26, it was maintained that "Badoglio and Victor Emmanuel are now the heads of the fascist state. The guard has changed. Our war against fascist Italy continues until the unconditional surrender of the armed forces of Italy, and the destruction of the fascist regime." On July 27, the OWI directive specified that "the king is not to be personally vilified, but he has to be referred to as a fascist." The characterization of Victor Emmanuel III in a broadcast as a "moronic little king" led to sharp reactions in the press because of its decidedly offensive tone, and Roosevelt himself had to disown the attack on the Italian king, maintaining that none of those responsible had been consulted.[53]

Actually, the mass media offered widely differing views on Mussolini's fall. The two most important newspapers had opposing views. The *New York Times* observed that the new government was simply a military dictatorship that had replaced another military dictatorship supported by a puppet king. The *Washington Post*, on the other hand, described Badoglio as an anti-Fascist and anti-German who enjoyed popular approval.[54]

The military commanders urged a nonideological reading of the situation. The fall of Mussolini came at the most opportune moment, when the landing was imminent, and General Eisenhower immediately took advantage of the occasion, using public opinion to achieve an armistice before the start of a landing on the peninsula in order to compensate for Allied military weakness. As Macmillan noted in his diary, Eisenhower summoned him at 8:00 A.M. on July 26 "in a great state of excitement and full of plans and ideas for exploiting the Italian situation."[55] A message to the Italian people was prepared in two days, as was a draft of what was later, after some corrections had been made, to become the "short armistice" with ten, later twelve, conditions for military surrender, to be issued in the event that the Italians took the initiative.

The two governments also modified the message to the Italians before it was broadcast on July 29. The original text was generally more positive with regard to the Italians. The promise to apply the Atlantic Charter's principle of self-determination to Italy was eliminated because, according to the British, it conflicted with the principle of unconditional surrender, but more so because it would have tied their hands with respect to territorial changes. Further, the commitment in the original text to return Italian prisoners was tied to Churchill's request that Allied prisoners be returned in order to prevent their deportation to Germany. There could have been extensive deportations after the announcement of the surrender. The prison camps scattered throughout Italy were thrown open, and thousands of Allied prisoners found refuge and assistance in Italian homes, in spite of the fact that concealing former Allied prisoners was punishable by death. Even with these modifications, Eisenhower's message was very convincing and effective:

> We commend the Italian people and the House of Savoy on ridding themselves of Mussolini, the man who involved them in war as the tool of Hitler and brought them to the verge of disaster. The greatest obstacle which divided the Italian people from the United Nations has been removed by the Italians themselves. The only remaining obstacle on the road to peace is the German aggressor, who is still on Italian soil.
>
> You want peace; you can have peace immediately, and peace under the honorable conditions which our Governments have already offered you. We are coming as liberators. Your part is to cease immediately any assistance to the German military forces in your country. If you do this, we will rid you of the Germans and deliver you from the horrors of war.
>
> As you have already seen in Sicily, our occupation will be mild and beneficent. Your men will return to their normal life and to their productive avocations, and, provided all British and Allied prisoners now in your hands are restored safely to us and not taken away to Germany, the hundreds of thousands of Italian prisoners captured by us in Tunisia and Sicily will return to the countless Italian homes who long for them.
>
> The ancient liberties and traditions of your country will be restored.

The reference to the House of Savoy was no coincidence. Eisenhower wanted to encourage the king to sue for peace and was convinced that the monarchy should be retained as a "symbol of Italian unity" until free elections were held.[56] Finally, it must be noted that both documents, the radio broadcast and the draft surrender terms, called for Italy's surrender, but not Italy's joining the Allied side, because Eisenhower was convinced that he could not ask the Italians for a decision he himself would consider to be against the code of military honor.[57]

Eisenhower's move to draft exclusively military surrender terms came at an opportune moment. The two Allied governments were still discussing the detailed draft prepared by the British and presented to the Americans in June, which lacked American approval.[58] The American Joint Chiefs of Staff and Roosevelt himself were against a detailed document that assumed de facto recognition of a central government in Italy. As has been seen, that would have been in stark contrast with the American interpretation of the principle of unconditional surrender, according to which the Allies must not deal with any central authority in the enemy country, since that would mean its recognition, but simply impose its own military administration. For the Americans, therefore, the Allied commander had to have the authority to deal with and possibly accept the Italian surrender. Roosevelt argued in a letter to Churchill of August 2 that it was better to confine negotiations to the short text, which Eisenhower already had. Eisenhower would be free "to meet situations as they arise," without having his hands tied by a document that could be "oversufficient or insufficient."[59] The American president repeated this position several times, both in subsequent discussions on the imposition of the long armistice on Italy and when the text for the German surrender was being drafted.[60]

However, his attempt to set the British text aside clashed with the firm determination of the Foreign Office, which declared its opposition both to limiting the Allied requirements to military conditions and to giving wider autonomy to the Allied commander. Eisenhower would have to transmit any armistice request to the two governments, which would make the final decision. Eden in particular insisted on presenting the Italians from the first with the political conditions prepared by his government. Churchill was then mediating between the Foreign Office's rigid position for imposing the full text and Eisenhower's milder one, which set a high priority on prompt action to convince the Italians to surrender. Churchill wrote Eisenhower that the text should not be "attractive and popular" but "cut and dried."[61] At the time he tried to soothe Eden, asking him to accept presentation of the short text, later to be followed up with the political conditions. In a note that was partially reported in his memoirs, the British prime minister tried to defuse the situation:

> Many things in life are settled by the two-stage method. For instance, a man is not prevented from saying, "Will you marry me, darling?" because he has not got the marriage contract, drawn up by the family solicitors, in his pocket. Personally I think the terms which Eisenhower may now offer are much more likely to be understood by an envoy, and thus be capable of immediate acceptance, than the legal verbiage of the Instrument of Surrender, and they will look much better if published. If we get emergency terms it means that the Italians will have given themselves up to us lock, stock, and barrel. There would be nothing improper in our requiring them to hand over the pull-through and other cleaning materials afterwards.[62]

The Foreign Office continued to disagree with the exclusion of political conditions, considering insufficient the addition of a final article that read, "Other conditions of political, economic and financial character that Italy will be required to meet will be issued later."

The lack of a common policy, and the differences between the British and Americans and the military commands and their governments regarding the attitude to assume concerning possible initiatives on the Italian side, were elucidated in a note of August 10, 1943, by Harold Macmillan. The note began with a request to explain the meaning of unconditional surrender:

> What is the meaning of the phrase "Unconditional Surrender"? It clearly cannot mean surrender without conditions because London and Washington have for four months been engaged in writing conditions which have already reached 42 clauses and are not yet finished.

Presumably, therefore, it means surrender on our conditions, surrender without bargaining. There is however a new refinement
which has been conceived which implies two stages – first surrender without even being allowed to see conditions; second, having
surrendered the conditions are shown to you. I do not know how
seriously this distinction is intended.[63]

Macmillan then asked what was the "general policy which I
should promote." He presented a series of questions to his War
Cabinet colleagues on the British government's goals and on the
actions they believed General Eisenhower should carry out in case
of an approach by an Italian military commander or a civil representative of the Italian government. He asked what surrender text
he should present, and so forth, showing the extreme confusion and
the contradictions prevailing in the Allied camp.

Only the arrival of the Italian emissaries made it possible to
resolve the situation, even though only momentarily. Having no
other way out, the Foreign Office was obliged to accept Eisenhower's
text, at least temporarily, while waiting for the American government to adopt the longer document. Agreement between Roosevelt
and Churchill was to be reached only at the Quebec Conference of
August 14–24, 1943. The final text of the long armistice, approved
on August 21, called for the surrender and total disarmament of the
Italian forces, Allied control of Italy and onerous economic conditions. Among other matters, Clause 29 on war criminals, which
required the arrest of Mussolini and the main exponents of Fascism
and their consignment to the Allies, was made definitive.

On the Italian side, the decision to contact the Allies was made
in an atmosphere of great uncertainty and confusion, and in the
absence of a specific plan. Contrary to what the Anglo-Americans
expected, the Italian government did not intend to request an
armistice immediately. In fact, the king was not prepared for unconditional surrender, just as previously he had hesitated before removing Mussolini. The mutual mistrust and internal divisions among the
military commands, especially between the Supreme Command and
the Army General Staff – and the excessive fear of German reactions
if any information leaked out about contacts with the Allies –

delayed a definitive choice on the means to depart from the war. Finally, from the moment he took office, Badoglio was faced with hostility in court circles, which considered him too weak with respect to the anti-Fascist opposition. The opposition was also divided on what to do. Although it did press the government to act, it deliberately remained inactive in order to leave the conclusion of the armistice to Badoglio. In the words of Alcide De Gasperi, leader of the new Catholic party, this was a "passive game" that inevitably placed heavy responsibilities on the negotiators.[64] Among the military, only Ambrosio stressed the urgency of reaching an agreement with the Anglo-Americans, convinced as he was by the arguments of General Giuseppe Castellano, who enjoyed Ambrosio's complete confidence and who for months had been insisting that the military should take the initiative.

The decision to initiate negotiations with the Allies or, better, to ascertain their intentions was made in a meeting at the Quirinal Palace in Rome on July 31 after the new foreign minister, Raffaele Guariglia, returned from his previous post in Ankara. Guariglia, like Badoglio, had made his career under Fascism and was ambassador to Spain during its civil war. He was certainly not the most appropriate person to promote a clean break with the past, and in fact he moved with leaden feet. The first emissaries were two diplomats, Marquis Blasco Lanza d'Ajeta, who was immediately sent to Lisbon, and Alberto Berio, who was dispatched to Tangier as consul general. The two had no mandate to open negotiations for an armistice, but were charged with sounding out the Anglo-Americans' intentions and requesting that they land in southern France or the Balkans, so that these diversionary operations would draw out the German divisions stationed in Italy.[65] Both men contacted British representatives and limited themselves to describing the difficult domestic situation and the danger of a popular uprising, as well as explaining that the Italian government needed to pretend to continue its alliance with Germany in order to avoid a German coup. Informing Roosevelt about Lanza d'Ajeta's conversation with the British ambassador in Lisbon, Ronald Campbell, Churchill stated that the Italian emissary had not made "any mention of peace terms," but only described the country's domestic situation, where there was no longer anything "between the King and the patriots who have rallied round him and rampant Bolshevism," and pressed an urgent request that "we should save Italy from the Germans as well as from herself and do it as quickly as possible," with an Allied landing in force on the peninsula.[66] Alberto Berio, after waiting for several days to be received, asked Campbell what the Allied peace conditions were. The response was a complete refusal of any discussion and a preliminary request for an unconditional surrender. Not even Eisenhower was informed of these preliminary contacts.

The real negotiations got under way only when the initiative passed to the military. After the Tarvisio Conference, where the Germans had clearly shown their intention to occupy northern Italy, Ambrosio made up his mind to take the initiative. He decided to send General Giuseppe Castellano, taking advantage of an Italian delegation that was leaving for the Portuguese capital on August 12. Castellano was sent without credentials, to prevent compromising documents from falling into enemy hands and to leave Ambrosio the option of disowning this action whenever it would appear useful.[67] Castellano, however, who was an enthusiastic supporter of the armistice option, went beyond his generic mandate to paint a picture of the Italian situation for the Allies and "advise a landing north of Rome, since otherwise the capital and the men in charge could face serious danger."[68] If he had done only that he would have faced the same wall of Foreign Office opposition, and the request for unconditional surrender prior to any discussion, as had all the other Italian emissaries. He was able to overcome this obstacle by maintaining in a meeting with the British ambassador in Madrid, Samuel Hoare, during a stop of a few hours on his way to Lisbon, that the real objective of the new Italian government was to transfer Italy to the Allied side, with the active collaboration of the Italian army against the Germans when the Allied troops landed in Italy. The Italians would accept unconditional surrender if they could "join the Allies in fighting the Germans."[69] The Italian government had not authorized Castellano to make such a statement, as Minister Guariglia noted to him on his return to Rome, but it was just this proposal, immediately sent by Hoare to the Foreign Office, that caused the Italian emissary to be listened to and that brought about a significant change of heart among the Anglo-Americans.[70] So that he would be taken more seriously, Castellano provided information on the deployment of German forces in Italy and asked to discuss the offer of military collaboration with Anglo-American officers.

Eden, informing Churchill of the arrival of the new Italian emissary when Churchill was in Quebec for a military conference with Roosevelt, continued to insist on a prior declaration of surrender of the Italian forces and favored a meeting between Castellano and an Allied military officer for the sole purpose of gathering information on German intentions and the location of their forces. He advised giving Castellano the same answer that was given to Berio:

> The Italian Government should place themselves in the hands of the Allied Governments, who will then state their terms, adding that the question of the assistance that Italy could give us against the Germans cannot be determined until after this has been done. Although at first sight this offer of co-operation sounds tempting I feel that if we accept it will land us in all sorts of difficulties both military and political with few if any corresponding advantages. If this judgement is correct I am sure we ought to stick to our present policy of refusing to make the Italian Government any promises or enter into any bargain with them in return for their surrender.[71]

However, Churchill and Roosevelt were deeply affected by the idea of Italy's changing sides, which they thought would save a good deal of time and bloodshed in the struggle against Germany. Convinced that some concrete Italian assistance was possible, they decided, in contrast to the Foreign Office view, not to insist on prior Italian acceptance of unconditional surrender. They asked Eisenhower to send two representatives from his headquarters in Algiers, and they sent to the Italian envoy both the text of the military armistice conditions and a written declaration prepared at Quebec. The "Quebec Declaration" announced that the armistice conditions did not call for "the active assistance of Italy in fighting the Germans"; any change in the armistice conditions would depend "on how far the Italian government and people do, in fact, aid the United Nations against Germany during the remainder of the war."[72]

The first meeting between Castellano, British Ambassador Ronald Campbell and the two generals Eisenhower had sent, the American Bedell Smith and the Englishman Kenneth Strong, held in Lisbon on August 19, was marked by mutual deception.[73] The Italian envoy maintained that his government wanted to change sides and have the Italian army collaborate in the struggle against the Germans after the Allied landing, whereas the idea had been discussed only with Ambrosio and only in a preliminary fashion. It had not even been discussed with Badoglio or Guariglia. The Anglo-Americans insisted on unconditional surrender, portraying their forces as overwhelming, with no need of foreign assistance. Actually, the Anglo-American officers thought it crucial to have Italian collaboration or at least neutrality to avoid the risk of failure at the time of the Salerno landing. General Alexander, who was in command of the operation, stressed several times to the Allied negotiators that the Allied military position was weak and that an armistice should be signed at any cost.[74]

Leaving Rome on August 12, Castellano was prevented by a series of mishaps from returning until the 28th and was unable to communicate with his government during that interval.[75] In the meantime, disagreements and suspicions within the Italian armed forces were such that Roatta and Carboni sent another emissary, General Giacomo Zanussi, to Lisbon "to balance and oversee Castellano's work,"[76] which made the Allies still more suspicious of Italian intentions. Zanussi was put under virtual house arrest after the British ambassador in Lisbon, on instructions from the Foreign Office, had given him a copy of the long armistice, whose text had in the meantime been finally approved by the two governments.

The Foreign Office hoped with this move to replace the short armistice with the long one. However, Eisenhower, fearing that the harsh long-armistice clauses would deter the Badoglio government from signing the surrender, asked permission to have only the military clauses signed, although promising to give the Italian emissaries the additional text after the signing of the armistice. Bedell Smith and Kenneth Strong took Zanussi with them to Algiers in order to prevent him from informing his government about the text of the long armistice.

4. The Signing of the Short Armistice at Cassibile and the Plans for Military Collaboration between Algiers and Rome

On his return to Rome, Castellano reported to Badoglio both the proposal he made in the government's name that Italy change sides and the Anglo-American emissaries' firm insistence on unconditional surrender. Badoglio decided not to repudiate Castellano's move and, thinking that there was still room for negotiations, gave him a mandate to present counterproposals. The talks continued at Cassibile, near Syracuse, Sicily, where Castellano traveled on August 31. There he encountered Zanussi, who for some inexplicable reason did not inform Castellano that he had seen the text of the long armistice.[77]

Even later, Zanussi did not seem to have realized that he was the victim of a deception and notes in his memoirs only that the Anglo-Americans gave him a series of contradictory directives. He underestimated the seriousness of the long armistice and in two messages to Rome demonstrated great optimism, maintaining that the political and military clauses had "a very relative value" and there should not be concern for the "unconditional surrender" which "was for the public."[78] In fact, in Algiers, Macmillan, to offset the negative effects that a knowledge of the text of the long armistice could have on the Italian decision to sign the surrender, tried to play down its importance and stated to Zanussi that the clauses of the long armistice should not be taken literally. Neither Castellano nor Zanussi was aware that the real reason the Allies insisted on an immediate signature was that the landing was imminent.

Castellano reported his government's conditions for changing sides, advancing a request for an Allied landing of fifteen divisions.

However, he received from Bedell Smith the revealing response that in that case the Allies would not need to conclude an armistice with Italy.[79] Castellano stated further that he was not authorized to sign the armistice without a prior commitment from the Anglo-Americans to land north of Rome. Until the very end he tried in vain to gain acceptance of his proposal to delay the announcement of the armistice until the major landing had taken place. The Anglo-Americans stated that these requests were unacceptable and insisted that the armistice be announced simultaneously with the beginning of the operation. Secondary landings would take place from one to two weeks before the announcement of the armistice. They were therefore elusive about the dates and allowed Castellano to be convinced that there was still time before the armistice was announced rather than conveying to him a sense of urgency, and they implied that the landings would be in force.[80] They were nevertheless clear on the fundamental points that the landings would be south of Rome and that the Italians would therefore have to protect the capital with their forces alone until the Allies arrived.[81]

The Allies spared no efforts to persuade the Italians to sign the armistice, subjecting them to continuous pressure to make up their minds immediately, passing from threats of air raids on Rome to an acceptance of Castellano's request to send an airborne division to help the Italians maintain control of Rome. In transmitting his decision to carry out this risky operation, Eisenhower argued in two messages to the Combined Chiefs of Staff of September 1, 1943, that Italy was "in fact an occupied country," at least north of Rome, and that sending this division constituted the only chance to convince the Italians to sign the armistice and to take Rome and all of Italy south of it with their assistance.[82]

Meanwhile, Castellano, who had returned to Rome the evening of August 31, was summoned by Badoglio on the following day, September 1. At this meeting, which also included Guariglia, Ambrosio and Carboni, Castellano reported on the conditions posed by the Anglo-Americans and gave Badoglio a copy of the minutes of the talks. According to this document, there would be "secondary landings (5 or 6 divisions) with Italian opposition. After a short interval (one or two weeks?) there would be a major landing south of Rome, the operation by the paratroop division near Rome, and at the same time the announcement of the armistice."[83] This account also reported the Allied refusal of the Italian request to concentrate the Italian fleet at the base at La Maddalena, Sardinia, as well as General Smith's statement that the landing would certainly involve fewer than fifteen divisions. After Castellano made his report, the meeting was divided. Ambrosio and Guariglia insisted that there was an alternative to accepting the conditions imposed. Carboni opposed this, because the Allies' verbal assurances could not be trusted and because his armored corps, whose mission was to defend Rome, could not fight the Germans "since it lacked fuel and munitions."[84] Badoglio did not give an opinion at the time, pending his meeting with the king, who had decided that afternoon to accept the conditions imposed. Thus the Italian government knew by September 1 that "the choice of the day for announcing the conclusion of the armistice remained at the discretion of the Allies"[85] and that concerted action was to commence at the time of the announcement, the assumption being that the Italians would be in control of the airports agreed on for the division's arrival and the defense of Rome against the Germans. On that day, Eisenhower informed the Italian Supreme Command of his decision to send "a large contingent of airborne troops to the area around Rome," provided that the Italians were in control of the required airports and that their divisions would undertake "active and effective military actions against the Germans and announce the armistice when requested."[86] Neither Badoglio nor Ambrosio thought it appropriate to inform Roatta of these agreements, at least according to the official account. However, it seems strange that Roatta was not informed by Carboni and that so delicate an operation continued to depend on Carboni after he had openly opposed it.

Castellano returned to Cassibile on September 2, but without a written authorization. Here too it is not clear whether Badoglio had tried to avoid a written commitment in the hope that the Anglo-Americans would not demand one. Instead, the Italian emissaries were relegated to a field tent pending the arrival of their authorization from Rome. This came on the afternoon of the 3rd, and an hour later the armistice was signed by Castellano and Smith in the names of Badoglio and Eisenhower, respectively. The photographs of this historic event convey a feeling of unease. Only Castellano and Montanari are in civilian clothes, among the Allied officers in uniform, and appear to have happened on the scene by chance. Castellano, in his dark suit with a white handkerchief in the jacket pocket, barely managing a half smile, seems to anticipate the haste with which he and the other generals would remove their uniforms on September 8. Immediately after the short armistice was signed, Smith handed Castellano the text of the long armistice, which had been given to Zanussi in Lisbon and then taken back by the Anglo-Americans.

In conclusion, it should be stressed again that both parties based their signing of the armistice on mistaken evaluations and judgments of the situation in Italy. Aside from the deception and mutual ambiguity concerning their respective forces, the principal error of judgment concerned the anticipated German reactions. Both the Allied and the Italian governments were aware of the German plan to withdraw to the Apennines in the event of a landing in force. The Anglo-Americans did not consider the fact that its implementation depended on the number of troops they would deploy on the Italian front. Actually, Marshal Kesselring was able to modify the withdrawal plan when he realized how few forces were involved in the Allied landing.[87]

During the negotiations and talks with the Allied representatives, the Italian side did not conceal the weakness of its army and the need for Allied support in fighting the Germans. Clearly the Anglo-Americans underestimated these indications to the point of being convinced that sending an airborne division would be enough to maintain the Italian control of Rome. Further, even though fearing that the Italians might double-cross them, the Allies believed Castellano's assurances that the Italians would fight the Germans. As General Alexander's biographer wrote, "The instrument of surrender, in fact an armistice, was also implicitly an instrument of alliance, for it presupposed Italian help against the Germans and

Allied help for the Italians."[88] On the other hand, the Allies believed that the six Italian divisions around Rome would be more than adequate to hold off the two German ones and protect the airports so the airborne division could land. The plans and forecasts of the Anglo-American military services in July–August 1943 indicated that their military leaders anticipated a "collapse" or "progressive disintegration" of the Italian forces even without a formal surrender and a German withdrawal. Given these circumstances, there was no doubt the Allies would soon reach Rome.[89] Castellano, for his part, became convinced that the acceptance of his request was evidence that the Allies would land in sufficient force to reach the capital soon, because otherwise the airborne division would be at serious risk.

The Allied representatives greeted the signing of the armistice with enormous relief. They had believed to the end that the Italians would change their minds. On September 3, right after the signing, Harold Macmillan wrote to Churchill: "The armistice conditions were signed this afternoon without amendment of any kind."[90] General Alexander also informed Churchill that Castellano "is remaining here near my headquarters and we are starting military talks this evening to arrange the best assistance the Italian forces can contribute to our operations."[91] After the armistice was announced, Castellano stayed at Cassibile to coordinate plans for military collaboration and establish which positions would be occupied by Italian units.

The account of the talks undertaken immediately after the armistice by the Allied military commands and the Italian representatives shows that Alexander was at first convinced that the Italians would be able to control their territory and oppose the Germans. The missions assigned the Italians were extensive and included direct attacks on the headquarters of German formations and units, interruption of communications, destruction of depots and aircraft, control of communications in the area around Rome and other measures to prevent German reinforcements from arriving. Finally, the Italians were requested to control the ports of La Spezia, Taranto and Brindisi.[92]

The initial optimism about effective Italian collaboration against the Germans soon subsided. In a message of September 4 to the British Chiefs of Staff, Alexander wrote: "The whole of last night was spent in military talks with Italian party. I have made it quite clear to them that on the official issue of the armistice we cease to be enemies but we are not, repeat not, allies. I have given them specific instructions to carry on which will help us in the sabotage line, sit down strike, forming guerrilla bands, etc."[93] Doubts about the possibility of the Italians carrying out these plans increased in the following days. On September 6, Alexander wrote: "There is a great deal of detailed planning going on between the Italians and ourselves. All this is going forward well in theory but we have still to see what actual help they will be able in fact to give us." And on the 7th, he announced that the final plans regarding "immediate operations in the Rome area, Avalanche and Taranto, were finally fixed." Finally, on September 8: "I had hoped that the talks our staff had with the Italians would at least have resulted in their preparations to receive and assist us, but I fear that despite our detailed instructions, they have done nothing."[94]

5. Actions Taken by the Italian Government and the Supreme Command from the Signing of the Armistice on September 3 to Italy's Surrender on September 8, 1943

Alexander's fears were to prove justified. Badoglio initiated nothing, in spite of the commitment made to defend Rome in cooperation with the British and Americans. He decided to keep secret the actual signing of the armistice from even his closest collaborators.

On the afternoon of September 3, Badoglio called a meeting with the ministers of the three armed services: Admiral Raffaele de Courten of the navy, General Antonio Sorice of the army and General Renato Sandalli of the air force. Joining them were General Vittorio Ambrosio, chief of the Armed Forces General Staff, and Duke Pietro Acquarone, minister of the Royal Household. Badoglio did not tell them that the agreement had been concluded, but only that negotiations for an armistice were under way. At the same time he furnished specific details about the operations planned by the British and Americans. This was in direct contrast to later statements by Badoglio and his armed services ministers that before September 8 they had known nothing of Allied intentions. Versions by other participants gloss over what was said at that meeting on September 3, but according to de Courten's account written a few days later, Badoglio had stated:

> The British and Americans will mount small-scale landings in Calabria, then a large-scale landing near Naples (six divisions), and finally a paratroop landing of a division near Rome, where Carboni's six divisions and the Italian 4th Army will be concentrated.[95]

This brief note from de Courten, a source not under suspicion, is of fundamental importance, because it refutes the network of lies constructed by Badoglio and the senior military leaders. It lists the information furnished by Castellano two days before, on September 1, and the commitments made by the Italians. It also confirms that Badoglio knew that the Allied landing was to take place south of Rome and verifies that this information was conveyed to the armed services ministers on September 3. There is no mention of further landings north of Rome.

The reference to the Italian Fourth Army indicates an assumption that the armistice would not be announced soon, since the Fourth was still very far from Rome, partly in Piedmont and in Liguria and as far away as France. In any event, once the government had decided to sign the armistice, knowing that Rome would be defended by only the six Italian divisions and the American airborne division, it should have issued the necessary orders to carry out the agreements into which it had entered.

Why were these orders not issued by either Badoglio or Ambrosio? The common explanation is that Badoglio decided to postpone action until the day of the armistice, fearing that the Germans might find out about it. However, in doing so Badoglio had decided from the beginning not to observe the commitments made by Castellano and to put at risk the American paratroop operation against Rome.

Meanwhile, at Allied Force Headquarters in Algiers, operational plans were being prepared for Giant 2, the code name for the landing of the paratroop division on the outskirts of Rome. On September 5, Major Luigi Marchesi, who had accompanied Castellano to Cassibile on September 2, returned to Rome to deliver important documents to Ambrosio: the text of the long armistice, a memorandum on the directives for the Italian fleet, which will be discussed later, and the operational order for the paratroop landing. This order anticipated Italian control of the air bases of Furbara and Cerveteri to allow the American division to land in three or four nights. At one point the Italian Supreme Command had specified the airports of Urbe, Centocelle and Guidonia, which were almost within Rome's city limits, but these were later eliminated from consideration as being too close to German antiaircraft defenses. A subsequent landing of an armored division at Ostia on the coast near Rome was also planned. This plan required neutralizing an area of about twenty kilometers on either side of the Tiber River. In addition to the documents, Castellano also sent a personal letter to Ambrosio stating that he had not been able to obtain specific information on the date of the main landing, but that "he thought it could be *assumed* that it would take place approximately on the 12th."[96] From then on, Ambrosio acted as if the landing could not take place before September 12 or 13, and he hastened to transmit this news to de Courten and Roatta.[97] At this point the versions of the various participants diverge, and an inaccurate report began to circulate that there would be fifteen British and American divisions, the number requested by Castellano in his conversation of August 31 and rejected by Bedell Smith in an almost derisory tone.[98]

The operational order for the paratroop division landing arrived on Roatta's desk the morning of September 6, together with a directive to provide the support and airport defenses necessary for executing it. It was only then that Roatta appears to have realized that "the Italian troops would have to initiate action against the Germans."[99] If it is true, as he maintained without being contradicted, that he had been ignorant of this plan until then, this discovery must have been quite a blow to him. For the Italians to neutralize the German troops on both sides of the Tiber and protect the parachute units after the armistice required complete control of the area, or taking the initiative on their own against the Germans, preventing them from occupying the airports for the three or four days necessary to complete the operation. By now five days had passed, but the Italians had still not made a move. Further, on that morning of September 6, Roatta deduced from the movement of landing craft from Palermo in Sicily to the coast of Salerno near Naples that a landing was being prepared there and that the announcement of the armistice was imminent.[100] That afternoon Roatta reported his concerns to Ambrosio, who remained convinced that no action would occur before September 12. Roatta also spoke with Carboni, commander of the motorized corps and chief of the Military Intelligence Service, who expressed the view that resisting for several days the German troops "who were *not engaged* at the same time against American troops" could not be considered.[101] Finally, even if none of the participants mentioned it, the announcement of an imminent landing came directly from the most authoritative source; on September 6, Allied Force Headquarters in Algiers sent a series of messages warning the Italian government to "maintain continuous watch every day for most important message," which would be sent "on or after 7 September," and other accessory information concerning "the announcement of the great Day."[102]

At this point the premise that the Italians would confront the Germans near Rome with no external assistance was definitively discarded. In a memorandum Roatta proposed that under these circumstances plans for a paratroop landing followed by the armistice announcement would have to be reexamined. Copies of the memorandum were left at the Supreme Command and with Carboni in his capacity as chief of Military Intelligence, who sent his copy to Badoglio.[103] Another memorandum was prepared at the Supreme Command on the basis of information from Roatta. It was delivered to Castellano on the evening of the 6th by Major Alberto Briatore, who had gone to Algiers with other officers to constitute an Italian military mission at Allied Force Headquarters. The Commission of Inquiry headed by Mario Palermo was later unable to find the text, but I located it in the Castellano papers.[104] This is a most important document, since it specifically mentions the "main landing by sea in the Salerno–Naples area," and therefore confirms irrevocably that the Italian command was aware on September 6 that the principal landing was to be in that vicinity.

During the inquest conducted by Mario Palermo, a heated controversy arose about these two memoranda, one written by Roatta and the other by the Supreme Command. Carboni delivered a document to the Commission of Inquiry, contending that it was a copy of the text sent to Castellano on September 6, which had been given him by the Supreme Command. The document differs in style but is very similar in substance to the one located in Castellano's papers, which requested a delay in the announcement of the armistice to a few days after "the attack by six divisions in the Salerno–Naples area." Carboni's testimony, if accepted, would have proved that the Italians were aware already on September 9 of the place of landing. The authenticity of the document was denied by Ambrosio and Roatta, who stated that it had been fabricated in order to discredit the Supreme Command. In the first instance Castellano and Rossi recognized the note as authentic. However, a few weeks later they asked the Commission to hear them again and denied knowing on September 6 that the landing was to be on the coast of Campania, near Naples.[105] It is probable that the text Carboni submitted was the memorandum Roatta had prepared the evening of the 6th, which is confirmed by the testimony of Colonel Vincenzo Toschi, who reported directly to Carboni. Carboni told the Commission of Inquiry that he recognized the document, written in Roatta's hand and typed by him on the evening of the 6th. Toschi also recalled that the text mentioned the landing area of Salerno–Naples and added an illuminating point: "Further, there had been a great deal of discussion about the Salerno–Naples landing, especially after the landing in Calabria."[106]

The Commission's persistence in pursuing the issue of the memorandum indicates how crucial it was to clear up the problem of which information the Italian Supreme Command was in possession of before September 8. The attempt to cover up the truth – the choice made on September 6 not to fight the Germans around Rome alone and not to collaborate with the British and Americans in Operation Giant 2 – was carried out awkwardly, but it achieved the desired result. The notion that the Italian Supreme Command was anticipating a landing near Rome and was taken by surprise on September 8 became the official version of events.

There is another important aspect of this matter. In spite of the differences among the Italian military leaders, the position taken by Roatta and Ambrosio at the Commission of Inquiry shows that both officers were united with Badoglio in his attempt to fabricate an alternative version and to hide their actions behind a wall of silence. The notion that Ambrosio wanted Italy to change sides but was prevented from this by Badoglio or Roatta was completely refuted. Therefore, the importance ascribed by the Commission of Inquiry to the Roatta–Ambrosio memorandum is justified. For this reason, the real memorandum was probably concealed from the commission.

The Italian leaders hoped to save the situation by requesting on September 6 a postponement of the announcement of the armistice, and they made one last attempt on the 8th. At the same time they were working on alternative plans to flee.

The extent of the Italian lack of preparation was discovered only on the night of September 7, when General Maxwell Taylor arrived in Rome on a secret mission. As commanding general of the paratroop division, he was accompanied by another officer on his mission of drawing up the final agreements and confirming the reliability of Castellano's assurances that the airports where the Allied paratroopers were to land were indeed in Italian hands. But the two officers realized to their astonishment that the only preparation made for them was a luxurious dinner. General Ambrosio had left for Turin on the preceding day, officially for the purpose of destroying some compromising papers.[107] The Americans could speak only with Major Marchesi and General Carboni.

When Taylor requested an inspection of the airfields and informed Carboni that the landing was scheduled for the following day, the Italian officer suggested that the operation should be post-poned or canceled, exaggerating the number of German troops around Rome and minimizing the number of Italian troops. Carboni also noted that the Italian divisions in Rome had no fuel, a scarcely credible excuse since it implied that the motorized corps deployed in defense of Rome was useless. Actually Carboni was deliberately deceiving, since he knew that there was a large fuel depot on the road from Rome to Ostia.[108]

Finding it difficult to believe Carboni and failing to understand how this reversal had come about, Taylor demanded to speak with Badoglio and arrived at the house of the marshal, who was sound asleep. Appearing in pajamas before his guests, the old marshal could only confirm Carboni's statements. On two occasions, in the two most tragic moments of recent Italian history – the night of Caporetto, a major Italian defeat in World War I, and the night of September 7–8, 1943 – the fate of Italy was entrusted to Badoglio and on both occasions he had gone to bed. At Caporetto, as a sub-sequent parliamentary inquiry revealed, Badoglio had failed to arrange appropriate artillery deployment and thus contributed to the rout of the Italian army. On the night before the announcement of the armistice, he professed to be "surprised at the rapid course of events" and unhesitatingly repudiated all the commitments made in his name by Castellano. He said that the American parachute landing and the announcement of the armistice would have to be postponed, given the lack of preparedness of the Italian forces.[109] The departure of the division was near, so that Taylor, after trying to make Badoglio understand the seriousness of the decision to with-draw at the very last minute, forced him to send a request directly to Eisenhower to cancel the operation. Badoglio stated in his message:

> Due to changes in the situation brought about by the disposition and strength of the German forces in the Rome area, it is no longer possible to accept an immediate armistice as this could provoke the occupation of the capital and the violent assumption of the government by the Germans. Operation Giant Two is no longer possible because of lack of forces to guarantee the airfields.[110]

In his memoirs, Badoglio gives a radically different version of this crucial document, in which he rejects the armistice and the sending of the airborne division and does not even request a postponement. According to Badoglio, "reconfirming the feelings of cooperation and loyalty on the part of the Italian government," he had in fact insisted "that the armistice take effect on the 12th."[111] Badoglio also contended that it was the Americans who decided to cancel the parachute landing. Badoglio's version has become the commonly accepted one, and it has been repeated in official military histories and by most historians.[112]

In these circumstances, the Americans had no choice but to cancel the operation only a few hours before it was to get under way. Military historians differ on whether Operation Giant 2 could have been carried out and what its chances of success would have been.[113] In this situation the operation would have been very risky, and there is no way to estimate what the consequences would have been. On the other hand, no one knew then what the Allied plans were, and the psychological effect on the German command of the division's arrival in Rome should not be underestimated. That might have been the only opportunity to force the Germans to withdraw north of Rome.

6. The Directives for the Italian Navy

In considering a landing in Italy, the Anglo-Americans had posed the problem of the still-intact Italian fleet and its use in case of a landing. Churchill had repeatedly emphasized the advantages that possession of the Italian fleet would give the Allies. The OSS looked on it as a "trump card," the decisive factor in any negotiations, and prepared a secret plan for its transfer to the Allies with the collaboration of Italian naval officers. This plan (the McGregor Project) was in the early stages of execution when Fascism fell.[114] On the Italian side, the destiny of the fleet was at the center of the negotiators' concerns from the first contacts with the Anglo-Americans. The latter, however, showed no willingness to make concessions. At Lisbon,

Castellano had sought to eliminate from the armistice text the consignment of the fleet to ports controlled by the Allies. However, the counterproposal to concentrate fleet units in Sardinia was rejected out of hand.

The Italian request was repeated in successive talks, but was never taken into consideration. It is not clear how many details of the negotiations Navy Chief Raffaele de Courten became aware of, but he was certainly among the first to be informed. According to his version it was on September 3, while according to Badoglio and Ambrosio it was at least two days before that.[115] With unfounded confidence, Ambrosio informed de Courten that the fleet would sail to La Maddalena, Sardinia, "where His Majesty would also go."[116] On September 6, however, Ambrosio transmitted to de Courten the *pro memoria* sent by Castellano that indicated the locations under Anglo-American control to which the fleet was to proceed at the time of the armistice announcement. The fleet at La Spezia was to proceed to Bone, Algeria, while the ships in Adriatic ports or Taranto were to proceed to Malta.[117] In response to de Courten's protests at so serious a situation for the navy, Ambrosio assured him again, saying that "the document can be regarded as a dead letter," because he had asked the Allies to let the fleet proceed to La Maddalena and that "there would certainly be no difficulties."[118] This request was found in the famous note of that same day, September 6, which Ambrosio sent to Castellano. However, Ambrosio's belief that the request would be granted is difficult to comprehend, since Castellano had already made that request in previous meetings where it had always been rejected.

De Courten could infer that the negotiations were far along from Ambrosio's September 5 request that two motor torpedo boats be sent to Ustica to meet two British officers and take them to Rome.[119] Nevertheless, despite these signs that the announcement of the armistice was coming soon, de Courten behaved to the end as if he would soon have to prepare the fleet for a final encounter with the traditional enemy.

CHAPTER THREE

September 8, 1943, and
Its Consequences

1. September 8 and the King's Flight

Protagonists' accounts September 8, 1943, are even more contradictory than those concerning other events of the period. It becomes impossible to clarify the individual responsibilities for "the full folly of the Italian Government and Supreme Command."[1] The irrational behavior of Admiral Raffaele de Courten, chief of staff of the Italian Royal Navy, between the signing of the armistice on September 3 and its proclamation on September 8 is one of many elements that is difficult to explain. The roles played by various other actors in this drama and their relations with one another remain unclear. Obviously, Marshal Pietro Badoglio, head of government, kept the king informed, but the other military leaders also knew more than they admitted. After the fact, almost everyone claimed to have been kept ignorant of the negotiations, as if they had all been afflicted by amnesia. General Antonio Sorice, the war minister, even stated that he was told of the armistice only on September 8. Sorice was lying, because he had at least participated in the meeting with Badoglio on September 3, mentioned earlier. Ambrosio himself claimed that he had informed Sorice of the signing of the armistice in early September and had told de Courten and Sandalli of the negotiations as early as the end of August. On the other hand, it seems highly unlikely that Ambrosio, who, as chief of the General Staff, saw the three armed services chiefs "nearly every afternoon," did not keep them informed of what was happening.[2]

And how is one to explain Ambrosio's mysterious disappearance during General Maxwell Taylor's visit when the General Staff should have been intensifying its preparations in view of the imminent announcement? Ambrosio, after all, had been the principal supporter of the armistice. And why did he return from Turin by train with Marshal Caviglia instead of accepting his subordinates' invitation to use an aircraft? It is clear that Ambrosio did not want to meet General Taylor. He did not show himself even on his return on the morning of September 8, and the reasons for his behavior remain incomprehensible. The attitude of General Mario Roatta, chief of staff of the army, is also contradictory. On the one hand, he took the initiative of sending General Zanussi, one of his own men, to participate in the negotiations. On the other hand, Roatta later claimed that he had been left out of every decision and knew nothing until the end – except that he intervened on September 6 to prevent the implementation of the agreements. What role did General Giacomo Carboni play? He was against the armistice from the beginning, yet he was assigned a mission crucial for pulling Italy out of the alliance with the Germans. All these unanswered questions and ambiguities make plausible the theory that the king and Badoglio continued until September 8 to keep both options open: either an armistice with the Anglo-Americans in case their landing was strong enough to force the Germans to withdraw, or a repudiation of the armistice and continued cooperation with the Germans. If the second option had been followed, it is likely that Marshal Ettore Caviglia would have replaced Badoglio, who would then be blamed for the negotiations with the Anglo-Americans. According to the testimony of Aldo Visalberghi, then a second lieutenant in the grenadier corps, some officers in the motorized corps had told him:

> ... the problem will be to see if they land in the north or the south. If they land in the north, we have to stay on good terms with the Allies. If they land in the south, we have to stay on good terms with the Germans.[3]

It appears certain now that the Badoglio government never even considered taking the initiative against the Germans, not only because it was convinced that there would be a major Allied landing, but because it believed, as did the Anglo-Americans, that the Germans would carry out their plans to withdraw at least to the Apennine Mountains if faced with an Allied landing. When it became likely that neither of these events would take place, Badoglio ruled out any combat against the Germans and deluded himself into thinking it was still possible to postpone both the planned Allied airdrop near Rome and the announcement of the armistice. He requested the postponement of both in his telegram of the evening of September 8, which has already been described. The following morning Badoglio, at Roatta's suggestion, decided to send a senior officer to Eisenhower's headquarters to explain the Italian situation directly. Roatta prepared a second memorandum to General Francesco Rossi, who departed for Allied Force Headquarters on the 8th, on the same aircraft that brought Taylor back to Algiers. The Italian command thought, or pretended to think, that a last-minute message would suffice to persuade Eisenhower to postpone the announcement.[4]

Rossi reached Algiers after the armistice had been announced, which meant that his mission was useless, but the text of the message is crucial for understanding the attitude of the Italian Supreme Command and the Badoglio government on various still-disputed issues. The memorandum does not mention a presumed intention of the Allies to anticipate the date of landing; it only states, "... the Italian side had the clear impression that the landing in the Salerno–Naples area would take place around September 12."[5] Further, the Italians assumed there would be a second large-scale landing, and they therefore requested that the announcement of the armistice be postponed until that moment. It was also suggested that it would be appropriate "not to have Italian hostilities against German troops start immediately after the armistice." The reasons given for this request were as follows: "It is important that the Germans take the initiative, as will almost certainly be the case, because then there would not be the slightest doubt among the Italian people and the troops about fighting against the Germans." Some marginal notes, almost certainly written by General Rossi during his trip, concerned the request to put off the landing by at least seven days, and the parachute drop by a further twenty-four hours, to "save the face" of the Italians.[6] A note at the end of the text refers to the fleet: "Fleet: its cooperation is important. Do not demand that it go to the ports. Scuttle. Better Sardinia." The document accurately reflects the position of the Badoglio government on September 8 and its choice of a passive policy in the hope of avoiding the German reaction it feared. The last notation further stresses the widespread conviction, often expressed by de Courten, that it would be difficult to make the commanders of Italian naval units accept the dispatch of the fleet to Malta, since they would consider it dishonorable.

On the morning of September 8, the government and the military leadership were aware that the armistice was to be announced that day, since General Taylor had explicitly stated so. Further, the Anglo-Americans gave another unmistakable sign that X-Hour was imminent by their massive air raids on Frascati, headquarters of Marshal Albert Kesselring, the German commander in Italy. The Allied representatives had informed Castellano of their intention to bomb Frascati on the day the armistice was announced in an effort to paralyze the German command structure. In Rome, the Italians received Eisenhower's negative response to their requests in the September 6 note, including the one to allow the fleet to proceed to La Maddalena, Sardinia. The American commander insisted that it was impossible "to change plans of operations because of absolute imminence of operation and date already fixed."[7] Neither Badoglio nor Ambrosio took these clear warnings seriously enough, nor did they take action until shortly after 5:00 PM that day, with the arrival of Eisenhower's response to Badoglio's request (sent the night before) to postpone the armistice. Eisenhower's message reiterated the decision to announce the armistice at the agreed-upon time of 6:30 PM and to reveal the agreements with Badoglio to the world if his government tried to back out. Eisenhower warned:

> I intend to broadcast the existence of the armistice at the hour originally planned. If you or any part of your armed forces fail to coop-

erate as previously agreed I will publish to the world the full record of this affair. I do not accept the message of this morning postponing the armistice. Your accredited representative has signed an agreement with me and the sole hope of Italy is bound up in your adherence to that agreement. On your earnest representation, the airborne operations are temporarily suspended. You have sufficient troops near Rome to secure the temporary safety of the city, but I require full information with which to plan the airborne operations. ... Failure now on your part to carry out the full obligations of the signed agreement will have the most serious consequences for your country.[8]

Moreover, a Reuters announcement publicized the news that Italy had withdrawn from the war. Only then was a meeting convened of the so-called Crown Council, as that historic meeting has been inappropriately designated. Attending were the king; the duke of Acquarone, minister of the Royal Household; General Puntoni; the armed services ministers Sorice, Sandalli and de Courten; General Carboni; Foreign Minister Raffaele Guariglia; General Ambrosio; and "a pale, worn-out Badoglio."[9] At Ambrosio's request Major Luigi Marchesi was summoned, since he had been with Castellano at Algiers and was best informed on the positions taken by the Anglo-Americans. Developments in the meeting provide further confirmation of the thesis that the king and Badoglio were uncertain to the end whether to accept the armistice. There are conflicting accounts concerning statements made at the Crown Council. However, all agree in substance that Carboni's proposal to renounce the armistice and with it Badoglio himself, and to continue the war on the German side, was supported by a majority of those present, in spite of Eisenhower's threats. At this point, Major Marchesi intervened and tried to bring the others back to reality. He argued that Italy could not turn back after signing an armistice document and still convince the Germans of Italy's good faith. Only then was it decided that the commitment to proclaim the armistice would be honored, and Badoglio went to the broadcasting station to read the text of the announcement.[10] Throughout the entire meeting, no one brought up the issue of the defense of Rome.

There are still many open questions about the decision by the Italian military and the Badoglio government to take a passive stance with respect to the Germans in accordance with the armistice conditions. The most obvious result of this course of action was the failure to defend Rome, on which all attention had been focused from the start, but this was only one episode among many serious incidents in the disintegration of the Italian army that followed the announcement of the armistice.

The conspiracy of silence, by which any prior information had been withheld from the subordinate military commands, continued up to the armistice. Roatta contends that during the night of September 8–9 he asked Ambrosio to issue the order to execute Memoria 44, but that Ambrosio refused to do so without Badoglio's authorization, since it would be "in contrast to directives from the head of government and to the radio announcement he had just made."[11] Badoglio produced two mutually contradictory accounts. He contended before the Palermo Commission that he had said, "We need to issue the orders, which have already been prepared, not only to General Ambrosio, but also to Generals Sorice and Sandalli, and to Admiral de Courten."[12] In testimony before the military tribunal in Rome in January 1947, which was marked by persistent lapses of memory and clear contradictions, Badoglio denied that such an authorization had ever been requested. He also claimed that he did not remember or knew nearly nothing about negotiations with the Allies, because "they concerned military operations." Badoglio furthermore maintained, among other claims, that "he did not know what plan had been prepared for submission to the Allies to begin negotiations and bring them to a conclusion, much less what action was to be taken by us and what assistance we anticipated from them."[13] Thus the head of government, Marshal Badoglio, maintained that he knew little about the armistice negotiations since they were outside his jurisdiction, while the armed forces chief of staff contended that he could not issue orders without permission from the head of government.

In conclusion, even on September 8, Ambrosio, Badoglio and Victor Emmanuel III maintained their initial position not to oppose the Germans and not to prevent them from sending an increasing number of troops to "defend Italy." They persisted in the hope that the Germans would withdraw and thought only of facilitating their operations, in a manner that was clearly irrational. During the night of the 8th, the Italian Supreme Command, realizing that Promemoria no. 21 addressed to all units directly subordinate to it – twenty minutes after midnight had not been received, broadcast order no. 24202. This directive summed up instructions for reacting against German violence and concluded, "In no case are you to take the initiative in hostilities against German troops." These instructions put the army in the worst possible position for facing inevitable German aggression, aggravating its uncertainty and disorientation. In the meantime, German intentions had become clear. General Carboni, in charge of defending the capital, moved from extreme optimism to extreme pessimism during the night of September 8. About 11:00 PM he warned Ambrosio that the German troops were withdrawing. An order was given to allow the Germans to pass through Italian-controlled areas, hoping they would withdraw. The only concern at the upper levels of the Italian government was to flee to territory under secure Italian control in order to avoid falling into German hands.

From his first contacts with the Allies, Castellano had raised the issue of transferring the royal family to a safe place when the armistice was announced. In the meeting of August 31, General Bedell Smith had suggested Sicily, while Castellano had mentioned Sardinia. The topic was taken up again in subsequent meetings but no definite conclusion was reached. The king's choice fell on Sardinia, which was under Italian control. On September 5, de Courten ordered two destroyers, the *Vivaldi* and the *Da Noli*, to be at Civitavecchia, on the coast near Rome, and to be prepared if necessary to take the royal family on board. On the night of the 8th, however, the Germans occupied the coast around Ostia, near Civitavecchia. The decision was therefore made to take the king to Pescara, on the Adriatic, since the Via Tiburtina, leading east out of Rome, appeared to be the only exit route that was free of German troops.

There are puzzling aspects to the way this flight was carried out. In spite of their fear of the Germans, the members of the royal party took no precautions to conceal their departure. The king, queen and crown prince left Rome about 5:00 AM on the 9th, in the usual car, flying the royal standard. Four or five other cars followed, with Badoglio, Acquarone and their officers, all in uniform. They could not have passed unobserved through any checkpoints, and in fact were stopped at one, which allowed them to pass.[14] Just as the royal family was leaving, Roatta gave instructions to the motorized corps to regroup at Tivoli in order to avoid exposing "the city and its people to serious and useless losses" – that is, Roatta issued an order not to defend Rome. He also commanded the divisions on their way to Rome to alter their route, hoping thereby to safeguard Via Tiburtina, where the sovereign and his suite were to pass.[15]

As Badoglio himself recognized, "The Military Command decided not to defend Rome, because it believed that the landing would take place far from the capital and because the paratroop division had not come."[16] The sequence of events and the manner in which they transpired lead us to suppose that the order for the division to regroup at Tivoli was issued simply to protect the king's flight. However, others have maintained that there was an agreement with Kesselring providing for the delivery of Rome in exchange for the undisturbed flight of the king and the government. This hypothesis was first suggested by Carboni, but given his lack of credibility and his cavalier and incompetent actions immediately before the armistice and on September 8 and 9, it was not taken seriously, until it reappeared in the studies by Ruggero Zangrandi and by Palermo.[17] According to SS Colonel Eugen Dollmann, who represented Himmler in Italy, Kesselring, following Dollmann's suggestion, decided to allow the Italian sovereigns to leave in order not to make the military situation worse.[18] Kesselring might have made this decision on his own without informing Berlin, simply to avoid resistance by the Italian army if the king were arrested. However, other factors appear to preclude the existence of an agreement.[19] On the night of September 8–9 the Germans were apparently undecided about whether to leave Rome. Kesselring was anticipating an Anglo-American landing, and if this were to take place near the capital he probably would have followed the orders to withdraw to the north. The German Embassy in Rome had burned its files and sent its personnel home. According to testimony from Lieutenant Colonel Giacomo Dogliani, chief of the liaison office between Kesselring and the Italian Supreme Command, this indecision lasted up to the morning of the 9th. Dogliani recalls that he paid a farewell call on Kesselring at 8:00 AM, during which his chief of staff, General Westphal, who was present, let slip the observation "You, Dogliani, should do us one more favor: persuade your headquarters not to oppose the withdrawal of the German troops from Rome and possibly to examine jointly the viability around . . ." but he interrupted himself because Kesselring gave him a sign to stop.[20] If confirmed, this testimony would show that there was no agreement and that Kesselring was seriously considering withdrawal from Rome. Only on the morning of September 9 was Kesselring informed that the Italian Supreme Command had decided not to defend the capital.[21] Consequently, he prepared to take control of the city. Despite the series of contradictory orders and General Carboni's two-day disappearance, the fighting continued inside and outside the town. In the area near Porta S. Paolo, civilians and soldiers fought side by side against German troops.

Immediately after the armistice was announced, the German Supreme Command issued the code word Achse (Axis) for the plan to be followed in case of an Italian surrender. German commanders immediately occupied strategic points and gave the Italian units in Italy and the Balkans the choice of collaborating or being disarmed.

In any event, it is probable that Ambrosio and Badoglio left their headquarters around Rome without orders, not because of lack of time to distribute them, but because they wanted to avoid a conflict with the Germans. The total lack of guidance, the absence of orders at the moment of the armistice and during the hours following it and the abandonment of the capital by the government and the Supreme Command could only give rise to chaos and to a general collapse.

A Nation Collapses

The Allies were using all their propaganda resources to urge the Italians to fight the Germans. Immediately after the armistice was announced, Admiral Andrew Cunningham, naval commander in chief for the Allies, broadcast instructions to the Italian fleet to proceed to Malta, while General Henry Maitland Wilson, commander in chief of Allied forces for the Middle East, broadcast orders to Italian troops in the Balkans and the Dodecanese Islands to proceed to the nearest ports.[22]

Most historians have written that the fleet fulfilled the armistice conditions immediately and proceeded to the specified ports. The facts, however, are completely different. As noted earlier, the navy was perhaps the least prepared of the armed services to receive the surprising and unexpected order to deliver itself to the enemy, even if it had been alerted to react to a German coup. As Admiral Giartosio wrote:

> . . . in forty months of a bitterly fought war, the Royal Italian Navy was subjected to much less interference from the fascist political authorities and the German commands than the other armed services, and . . . on the other hand, England, which controlled the seas, had always been the traditional enemy, although that country was highly esteemed and admired. The about-face imposed by the armistice could therefore not be alleviated by anti-fascist or anti-German feelings, and had to be accepted, with no mitigating factors, as the humiliating gesture of the vanquished who lays down his arms before the enemy. The gesture was all the more painful and difficult because the navy was still combat-effective.[23]

The Italian navy moved with extreme caution:

> On the evening of the 8th, after the telegraphic orders had been issued, we could still explain the situation by telephone to the naval bases at La Spezia and Taranto. It was stressed that the strict observance of the armistice clause would be an important factor in the treatment given our country by the victors.[24]

De Courten, perhaps because he feared being disobeyed or because he was himself opposed to such a decision,[25] chose not to make an immediate request that the fleet carry out the armistice terms, as was clearly indicated by the series of radio messages sent from the evening of the 8th and throughout the 9th.[26] They show further that naval headquarters ordered the cessation of hostilities and the transfer of the fleet to the ports of destination just after the armistice was announced. Orders to proceed to Malta were transmitted only to Fifth Division Headquarters at Taranto. The naval squadron at Tirreno was first ordered to execute Promemoria no. 1 and then to regroup at the island of La Maddalena off Sardinia, where it was to receive further orders. At noon on September 9, the squadron was approaching the island when an order was received to change course and proceed to Bone, Algeria, since La Maddalena had been occupied by the Germans. While the ships were changing course, German aircraft bombed them, sinking the flagship, the battleship *Roma*, and causing numerous casualties. Indicative of the prevailing view in the navy is the fact that the attack was originally attributed to the British.[27] Only then did the fleet proceed to Malta. The fact that the minister of the navy continued to maintain contact with the ships, recalling that the fleet was to continue to fly the Italian flag in accordance with the armistice and that it was not to be demobilized, helped to maintain discipline in most cases. Not all of the fleet proceeded to Malta and many ships were lost, but with a few exceptions scuttling the ships was avoided. Overall, about half of the fleet was saved. Some units proceeded to the Balearic Islands, and nearly all of the merchant marine remained in the ports. However, given the situation, the results were satisfactory.

The misunderstandings and ambiguities that arose during the negotiations between the Allies and the Italians continued even after the armistice was announced. Badoglio, the king and the Italian Armed Forces General Staff were convinced that the landing at Salerno was "secondary," as Smith had described it to Castellano, and that the main landing would involve approximately nine divisions in an area near Rome. Even at the moment of the flight from Rome, they believed that this emergency would last only a week or two; after that, they expected to return to the capital, then in Anglo-American hands.

The king and Badoglio were certain their absence from Rome would last only a few days. According to the duchess of Bovino, of whom the sovereigns and their party were dinner guests on September 9 while awaiting to embark at Ortona, the king stated that Roosevelt had announced Italy's unconditional surrender only as "a campaign stunt" and, showing his wallet with only 1,200 lire, worth about 12 U.S. dollars at that time, said he was sure he would soon be back in Rome. For his part, Badoglio claimed "I am Piedmontese and if I say something it is because I am sure of it. We will be back in two weeks at the latest." Acquarone was convinced he would be back in three days. He had nothing but the clothes he was wearing.[28] This is one more indication of how far removed from reality the upper levels of the government were.

This optimism was to fade away in the following weeks. In a letter of October 19, 1943, Ambrosio reproached Castellano for his statement in the days before the armistice that "the capital would be in crisis just a few days before the arrival of the Anglo-American armies." In a marginal note Castellano observed that his statement related "to the defense of Rome and the use of the American paratroop division, which was not granted by the General Staff."[29] Neither the Italians, Churchill, Roosevelt nor Eisenhower could foresee that the Germans would hold Rome for nine months more, and perhaps that expectation was beyond the optimistic view of Kesselring. At the time of the landing, the Anglo-Americans expected to be in Rome by October, and in October they thought they would be there in November.[30]

September 8 revealed the fear of German reaction, an attitude that had paralyzed the government for the entire period following Mussolini's fall. The king and Badoglio continued the extremely prudent tactics employed up to then, supposing that the Germans would withdraw if they were not provoked. There was never any intention of engaging in active hostilities against the Germans, even when Italian military forces would have been sufficient. There are various reasons or combinations of reasons for this attitude, from the desire not to betray an ally, to the hope of "saving face," as was shown in General Rossi's previously mentioned note in the margin of the document he brought to Eisenhower on September 8, to the terror at German action against the population and the cities. In any case, the result was the disintegration of the Italian armed forces, the internment of 700,000 officers and men and the German occupation of nearly all of Italy.

2. Italy and Its Army in the Face of German Reaction

September 8 was a watershed for all Italians, military and civilian alike, even if it assumed a different, and sometimes opposite, meaning, depending on one's political orientation or individual experience. As Claudio Pavone has noted, "... even today, to look on September 8 as a tragedy or the beginning of a liberation process is a line that separates interpretations by opposing schools."[31]

With only a few exceptions, Italians greeted the armistice announcement with enthusiasm and relief. Many accounts gathered by Pavone show a series of responses, ranging from incredulity to astonishment to joy, then to concern and bewilderment as the real personal and national situations became clearer.[32]

These reactions followed one another rapidly at all levels. Once again, just as on July 25, the population interpreted the Badoglio government's decision to surrender as the end of the war. Church bells rang out in many cities; there was dancing in the streets, or more simply toasts and dinners among friends and relations. Most of the population hoped that it was all over and that normalcy would return, or at least that there would be no more hunger. These early expressions of happiness and the illusion that the Fascist adventure would come to a harmless conclusion soon gave way to concern for the immediate future. What would the Germans do? The answer was not long in coming, because the German response was immediate, with the execution of previously written plans for occupying the cities. On the Italian side, the army garrisons throughout the peninsula and the divisions occupying Yugoslavia, Greece and Albania were immediately faced with the problem of what to do. Badoglio's proclamation ruled out any organized resistance and left the armed forces units without instructions. His ambiguous directive to react to "any attacks from any source" clearly referred to the Germans, but excluded any Italian initiative. The failure to order the enactment of Memoria 44 aggravated the situation. The commanders' passive attitude and inability to assume responsibility had disastrous results. After having waited in vain for orders from Rome, most of the generals and other senior officers in the various military units left surreptitiously. In many cases the soldiers were confined to their barracks, where they were taken prisoner by the Germans. In others they were given leaves or invited to disband and "go home." This constitutes one important difference between what occurred in Italy and what took place among the troops stationed outside Italy, where there was no disbandment because there was no "home" to go to. The choice of either surrendering to the Germans or continuing to fight was clearer from the beginning. Hence, among the troops outside Italy the instances of collusion with the Germans were more frequent, as were the acts of genuine heroism, such as the well-known case of the "Acqui" division at Cephalonia, where the decision to resist rather than lay down their arms was taken after a referendum among the officers and troops, in spite of the fact that the orders received called for the division to be disarmed.

In Italy, the bewilderment caused by the sudden change of front and the lack of preparation for it resulted in most cases in a passive acceptance of being disarmed by the Germans, in the vain hope, supported by assurances from German commanders, that there would be no further offensive actions. However, the Germans began immediately to assemble the soldiers and transport them in armored cars to internment camps in Germany. An officer of that period wrote, "We were ignominiously betrayed [by the Supreme Command] and given over to the Germans."[33] When the trains loaded with soldiers and Allied prisoners who had not been able to escape from the camps began to proceed north toward the Brenner Pass on the way to Germany, the population tried to help the passengers: ". . . women, children, old people and railroad workers tried with unselfish energy and abnegation to rescue the men from deportation. Many cars were unhitched from their trains during the trip and locomotives sabotaged when being resupplied at the stations."[34]

In the general confusion, the military leadership was uncertain what to do, issuing orders, only to cancel them later. The testimony on these days tends to support the words of a soldier in the account of events by Fenoglio:

> And then they could not even give us any clear orders. There was a flood of orders, but each one was different or the opposite of the others. Resist the Germans; don't fire on the Germans; don't let the Germans disarm you; kill the Germans; lay down your weapons; don't give up your weapons.[35]

In some cases, commanders took the initiative and prepared defensive actions, with the support of the soldiers, but they had to desist in the face of the order to "leave free passage to the Germans and collaborate with them as far as possible."[36] There is no systematic study of the conduct of the various divisions, so one can get some idea of what went on only from unit diaries or individual testimonies. However, it would be a mistake to overgeneralize, as is usually done, and conclude that the entire army disintegrated without resistance. There were cases of resistance, especially in garrisons where the Germans arrived later, by which time it had become clear that they intended to intern Italian soldiers, and when the Germans were particularly violent.

In some other cases, the lack of direction was overcome immediately, generally through the capability and authority of a given commander. At Gorizia, Trieste, Cuneo, Savona, La Spezia and Viterbo, several garrisons refused to hand over their weapons to the Germans. They opened fire and resisted sometimes for long, sometimes for short periods. The German records speak of "sharp clashes" and stubborn resistance in various cities; German military sources also mention that in Turin "a Communist revolt was bloodily suppressed." On September 10, 1943, the Supreme Command of the Wehrmacht ordered that "in those localities where Italian troops or other armed elements offer resistance, an ultimatum should be issued making it clear that the Italian commanders responsible for the resistance will be shot as francs-tireurs if they do not order their subordinates to hand over their weapons to the German units immediately within the established time."[37]

In the Abruzzi, where the Legnano division disbanded, and in the Marche, there were only occasional clashes between German and Italian forces, as happened at Ascoli Piceno. The presence in these regions of a large number of disbanded soldiers and of Allied prisoners of war who had escaped from the camps located in those areas gave rise to the first partisan bands made up of military personnel. These were joined by civilians intending to defend their own homes and towns. With the arrival of Germans in larger numbers it was in these areas that the first reprisals were carried out at the end of September and the beginning of October 1943, as at Bosco Maltese and at Colle San Marco.[38]

In Rome the fighting lasted for two days with the assistance of civilians, until the agreement between Kesselring and the city military command became known.

On the other hand, in some places there was total inertia, or senior units deserted their posts, as in the case of the Seventh Italian Army, deployed over an extensive territory that included Campania, Calabria and Puglia. In this area, so crucial for the struggle then taking place following the Allied landings, first in Calabria on September 3 and then on the 9th at Salerno, the Italian troops were between the Germans and the Anglo-Americans, with no previous guidance and no orders after the armistice was announced. General Mario Arisio, commanding the Seventh Army with headquarters at Potenza in the southern region of Basilicata, decided to transfer part of his command to Puglia, where most of his mobile forces were located, as soon as he was informed that the armistice had been declared. He left the remaining units under his command in Calabria without orders. Arisio and General Raffaele Pelligra, his chief of staff, were investigated for their conduct. Concluding the investigation, General Giovanni Messe, then chief of the Armed Forces General Staff, summed up the events:

. . . departure was at midnight; in the meantime no operations were performed aside from the request to the Army General Staff for permission to move. There was no communication; no contact of any kind was made with the three subordinate corps . . . the transfer of tactical headquarters was executed in such a manner that there were no communications aside from the telephone when it reached its new location. Radio communication was established only on the morning of the 9th.[39]

In Messe's judgment, ". . . since this disorderly and hasty transfer had no technical justification, this gives rise to the suspicion that it was suggested by other concerns that certainly do not work to a soldier's honor."[40] Potenza had to cope with several German divisions passing through and was subjected to a massive Allied air raid that caused serious damage to the city and many deaths, among the military as well. Faced with the German order to surrender, Colonel Giovanni Faccin, the deputy chief of staff, who had stayed behind in command of the garrison, blankly refused and committed suicide on September 13 rather than surrender.[41]

Nor were the military units in a position to deal with the situation in the area around Naples. The behavior of General Riccardo Pentimalli, commanding the Nineteenth Corps with headquarters at Santa Maria Capua Vetere, General Ettore Del Tetto, who headed the territorial command, and General Ettore Marino was totally irresponsible. These men were charged with the defense of Naples but abandoned the city to the Germans even though there were ". . . enough forces and weapons for them to resist and operate in such a way that the army would come out of this serious situation with dignity and honor." And so

various units were left to themselves; the soldiers left their weapons and deserted; the barracks were looted by the people and the soldiers themselves; and the officers put on civilian clothes and fled.

The behavior of General Del Tetto and other senior officers was described as follows:

... he did not take all measures necessary to control the situation, and did not give clear orders to the commanders of his subordinate units. To anyone who saw him, he gave the impression of a man seized with fear. . . . General Del Tetto . . . accepted the German demands, even to the extent of releasing German prisoners along with the weapons taken from them while fighting in the city. When the situation became more serious, he left headquarters that afternoon without leaving any telephone message for his subordinate commands, and then disappeared. The troops of General Marino, who "enjoyed little trust and even less prestige," surrendered to the Germans "without firing a shot." General Riccardo Pentimalli "arrived in Naples so late that the situation had already deteriorated beyond repair and, following the example of General Del Tetto, he disappeared with his chief of staff and returned to Naples on October 1, the day the Anglo-American troops arrived."[42]

In spite of the total absence of direction the fact that many garrisons were practically immobilized by the lack of transport, tanks and antiaircraft weapons, several units led by decisive officers did attempt a defense of their positions, but were eventually overcome.[43] Even the civilian population was willing to join the soldiers in the defense of the city against the Germans, as became apparent when the people in Naples took the initiative during the German withdrawal.

In these cases it was primarily the lack of clear guidance from headquarters and the incompetence and disorganization of the local commands, as well as fear of the Germans, that led to the disintegration of the army. In very few cases was the collapse caused by an "ideological" refusal to fight a former ally or to go against personal convictions. However, there were some more politicized units in which a strong esprit de corps prevailed. Other such units had close connections and had operated with the Germans. Consequently, they looked on the armistice not with relief, but as a dishonorable abandonment of the alliance with Germany. Some units decided to continue fighting on the German side. For example, the tactical group of the "Nembo" paratroop division, stationed in Sardinia, under the command of Major Mario Rizzatti, defected and followed the German troops in their withdrawal from the island. Several officers of the division were Fascists and had carried out propaganda activities among the soldiers. Moreover, commmon experiences with the German "Langerhausen" division had led to comradely ties and a feeling of solidarity. Some of the troops had in fact fought with the "Folgore" division in Africa, side by side with the Germans. In a report written a few months after these events, the division commander, General Ercole Ronco, recalled that on the evening of September 8, when the news of the armistice spread through the division, "a sense of heartbreak and grief pervaded everywhere. The peripheral units constantly requested confirmation, in the hope that the news was not true and had been transmitted for propaganda purposes by irresponsible elements."[44] After the initial crisis, the majority recovered, but some feared losing "the halo of glory and sacrifice" for which they had joined the armed forces and dreaded "ending life miserably, without any further fighting." They listened to rebellious leaders, who anticipated the possibility of "giving up our weapons to the Americans, internment in concentration camps until the end of the war," and influenced by German propaganda, they decided to follow the Germans. Some defected because they were convinced that the entire division was going to do so, and others joined the rebellion in order to leave the island. The seriousness of the episode is shown by the murder of the chief of staff of the "Nembo" division, Lieutenant Colonel Alberto Bechi, who had gone to the dissidents in an attempt to persuade them to turn back.[45] The crisis spread to other formations, and there were cases of disintegration and open acts of rebellion, which the leaders, however, were able to restrain. In any event, approximately 600 men were involved.

According to some sources, the proportion of Italian to German troops in Sardinia was approximately 120,000 to 25,000–30,000; according to other sources, it was 200,000 to 15,000–20,000. The disparity of forces had led the Supreme Command to take for granted that the island would remain in their hands. In Memoria 44 the Italians had anticipated overpowering the German contingent.

On September 8, Admiral Bruno Brivonesi was summoned to Rome and informed of King Victor Emmanuel III's intention to sail for La Maddalena in Sardinia on ships of the First Squadron. As de

Courten later specified, naval headquarters "left it up to Admiral Brivonesi to decide what action to take on German requests for free passage in Corsica, but in substance he was authorized to facilitate it."[46] During the night of September 8–9, General Antonio Basso, who commanded the armed forces in Sardinia, requested permission to allow the German troops to withdraw from the island, and this was granted by the Supreme Command. However, on September 9, the Germans seized La Maddalena, breaking their commitment to leave peaceably just when the Italian fleet was proceeding there. The German action, executed by numerically very inferior forces, was very serious but Admiral Brivonesi, accepting the German explanation that the occupation was necessary to protect German troops in Corsica and that it would be limited to a few days, did not oppose it. In spite of this and other acts of violence against military installations on the island by the retreating Germans, General Basso did not change his policy of temporizing, in the expectation that the German forces would leave the field. Only after repeated urging from the Supreme Command did he begin on September 15 to "pursue" the German army, which by then was at Palau concluding the transfer to Corsica.[47] In contrast to their commanders' passive attitude, soldiers and sailors at La Maddalena spontaneously opened fire on the Germans, taking several prisoners. Officers managed to put down the "rebellion" with difficulty only after the Germans had agreed to replace the German guard, which de facto held Admiral Brivonesi[48] and his officers hostage, with one of Italians.

Thus General Basso in Sardinia disobeyed his orders and allowed the Germans to leave the island undisturbed. In Corsica, the situation was similar: Italian forces were deployed over the entire island, with inadequate weapons and little transport, and there was widespread demoralization. General Giovanni Magli, the commander of the Italian armed forces on the island, and his units behaved in an entirely different way. Magli applied Memoria 44 literally. At the first German attack on the port installations in Bastia on September 9, the Italian forces reacted decisively, passing from neutrality to open conflict. In the following days and weeks, attempts to reach agreement were interposed between other bouts of fighting for the control of Bastia. This lasted until the complete liberation of the island, in which the Italians participated, collaborating with Corsican partisans and then with the French, who had landed.[49] The different attitudes of these two generals cannot be explained on the basis of their political beliefs, since both had good relations with the Germans and Magli had "a bad reputation"; that is, he was considered so Fascist and pro-German, that after July 25 the possibility of relieving him of the command of the armed forces in Corsica had been taken into consideration.[50]

Another singular situation arose in Alto Adige, a region regarded by the Germans as of primary importance for the control of the Brenner Pass. From July 25 on, German forces had continued to enter through this pass in preparation for a possible occupation of the country. The Germans had flanked the Italian formations at all strategic positions and held the other passes in force. As in the rest of Italy, German organization and promptness were met by Italian uncertainty and confusion. Furthermore, from the first moment on, the German-speaking population in the region, increasingly alienated by twenty years of attempted Italianization by the Fascist regime, aligned itself with the German side, so that the Italian troops suddenly found themselves in enemy territory. Only a few detachments put up a weak resistance. The others surrendered to the Germans, who immediately loaded them onto trains heading toward the Brenner Pass on their way to Germany.

The worst possible combination of events happened on September 8. As already noted, the reigning chaos and confusion, the power vacuum and the near certainty of impunity enabled people to plunder at will. In one of his stories, Italo Calvino describes the recollections of September 8 by a group of soldiers during the Italian Social Republic:

> The favourite topics of conversation among the soldiers were about what they had taken away "on September 8" and how they had hidden it and kept it from the other soldiers and the Germans, and the money they had made selling it. The yellow-faced mule driver, who had not even stolen a blanket, sat silent, ashamed, while a former waiter from San Remo told of how he had escaped with ten

British pounds in gold in his athletic supporter. Envy turned to hatred of the officers since they had been able to make off with the regimental cash boxes, without dividing it up with the troops. When the next "September 8" comes, someone said, we will be more alert. And they dreamed up plans and castles in air on what they would be able to take at the second "September 8," about the millions they could earn.[51]

There are numerous stories of simple soldiers filled with rancor against the officers who had abandoned them or delivered them over to the Germans. In letters from soldiers during the two following years, the memory of the "many generals who betrayed Italy without fighting" was to remain vivid. One of them states:

> ... our officers ... still do not realize that they were the ones to have brought us to this, but I still remember that I was abandoned on September 8, 1943, by a cowardly captain and a foul warrant officer in the Carabinieri who left me in the clutches of the Germans. Now they claim our respect; when I see officers I feel like spitting in their face.[52]

German soldiers immediately began acting like occupation troops in an enemy country, giving themselves over to looting and violence. In areas where they were withdrawing, such as Calabria and Puglia, they destroyed everything that could possibly help the Allies' advance, with virtually no opposition from the Italian Seventh Army. They confiscated vehicles and cattle and plundered civilians. At Andria and Corato they extorted a "big ransom."[53] The only important action against the Germans by a senior officer in the Seventh Army area was taken by General Bellomo, who managed to prevent the destruction of the Port of Bari, driving off the Germans.[54]

3. The Italian Troops Abroad

When the armistice was signed, only twenty-four Italian divisions found themselves on Italian territory, while thirty-five divisions were occupying parts of the Balkans and of the Aegean Islands. Often situated in isolated garrisons, these occupational troops were scattered throughout vast areas, defending the coastline and fighting the partisans. The vicissitudes of the Italian forces abroad in the aftermath of the armistice and the tragic fate of many of those units that tried either to negotiate their surrender or to offer resistance, sometimes a prolonged one, to the Germans merit a brief discussion.[55]

The intense exhaustion experienced by the Italian occupational troops was exacerbated by partisan aggressiveness and the mutual mistrust between them and their German ally, which was taking possession of an increasing number of areas occupied at first by Italians alone. Between June and July 1943, the commanders of some units in Greece, the Aegean and Yugoslavia had attempted to clarify Allied intentions in case of their surrender, establishing contact through intermediaries with the British missions. Their initiatives were taken seriously to the extent that, as we have seen, they were the subject of letters between Roosevelt and Churchill; on the other hand, the request to surrender to the British and not to the partisans as well as the offer to collaborate with the British against the Germans fell into a void in the face of the categorical response of the Allied commands that "the surrenders must be unconditional."[56] The rigid application of the unconditional surrender principle prevented any contact before the announcement of surrender and any collaboration against the Germans.

The Italian divisions in the Balkans and the Aegean were completely in the dark as to developments in Italy and were taken by surprise by the announcement of the armistice, which for the most part they heard about on the radio.

There was no assistance from Italy, or from the Allied Middle East command. Among the agreements included in the armistice was an Allied commitment to convey back to Italy the Italian troops in the Balkans, who had to be warned by the Italian Supreme Command to move to the coasts. Immediately after the announcement of the armistice, General Henry Maitland Wilson, commander in chief of the Allied forces in the Middle East, issued a directive to Italian troops in the Balkans and the Aegean to proceed to the nearest ports.[57] However, not even that order was transmitted by the

Italians. Ambrosio later excused his silence and inertia with respect to the troops outside Italy in that crucial time by maintaining that "the race to the ports" was so obvious that it could be logically supposed that it would be carried out without specific orders from the commanders of the army groups.[58]

Actually "the race to the ports" did take place; it was blocked by the Germans and the partisans themselves, and there was a total lack of coordination with the Allies. Only a small part of the Italian army was able to save itself. In many cases, once the Italian troops had reached the coast after long, exhausting marches, they waited in vain for the arrival of the ships. Often, they were captured by the Germans or sought refuge in the mountains.

The divisions underwent different experiences, depending on the circumstances and on the individual commanders. Most of the units surrendered almost at once; others tried to negotiate the surrender of their weapons, in the hope of being repatriated; only a few accepted the German offer to continue the fight at their side. As in Italy, the Germans used force when they outnumbered the Italians, but were prepared to act with deception when the Italians had superior forces. They promised to repatriate the Italian troops in exchange for the laying down of their arms. Once the Italian units had been disarmed, the Germans failed to keep their promise and interned the Italians immediately or sent them to Germany. The Italian divisions stationed in the Aegean and the Dodecanese Islands gradually fell into German hands.

On some islands – Rhodes, Coo, Lero, Simi and Samos – the British were able to land some reinforcements. The small number of troops employed and the complete lack of prior coordination with the Italian forces, the persistent mistrust of them and finally the absence of assistance against the German air raids led to the failure of those operations. The Germans took Rhodes after a few days in spite of the superiority of the Italian forces. That island had great strategic value because its air bases would have enabled the Allies to regain control of the Aegean.

On other islands the Italians offered strong resistance, and once they surrendered, the officers and some of the troops were immedi-

ately shot. Santorino was the last island to be attacked and taken by
the Germans, in November. Cephalonia and Corfù, where the greatest massacres occurred, surrendered, respectively, on September 22
and 25. The Germans were afraid that Corfù and Cephalonia, close
as they were to Italy, could be used by the Allies as a bridgehead
toward the Balkans, according to a presumed "strategic plan" by the
Allies to gain total control over the Mediterranean.[59] Thus they subjected the two islands to heavy bombardment before landing in force
and used brutal violence in suppressing the Italian Resistance. In the
case of Cephalonia, the Supreme Command of the German armed
forces issued orders "not to take any Italian prisoners."[60] Hitler's
orders were fully carried out. About 1,300 of the "Acqui" division
died in combat or were killed when they fell into German hands and
about 5,000 were executed after they surrendered. Finally, 1,350 men
died in the sinking of the ships taking them to Germany, which were
bombarded by Allied aircraft. At Corfù, about 600 to 700 men died
in combat or were shot. Those responsible for these massacres were
judged to be war criminals at Nuremberg.

The choice of the Anglo-Americans not to send help when their
forces were only sixty miles away in Puglia had tragic consequences.
The Allied aircraft appeared only after the surrender, and bombed
the German ships loaded with Italian prisoners. As we will see,
Churchill in the following weeks continued to press the case for
landings on the islands, especially Rhodes, but at that point the
American leaders were firmly opposed.

In Albania, Yugoslavia and Greece, many preferred to take
refuge in the mountains and join the partisans rather than surrender to the Germans. However, they did not always get a favorable
reception, and many units and lone soldiers were massacred. In
Yugoslavia, a large part of the "Taurinense" alpine division and the
"Venezia" infantry division, with the exception of the militia formations from the latter that went over to the Germans, joined Tito's
partisans and made up the "Garibaldi" division, which fought until
the end of the war with the popular Yugoslav army, although relations were difficult and there were several instances of violence on
the part of the Yugoslavs.

4. The Allied Reaction to the Disintegration of the Italian Army

September 8 was also a turning point for the Anglo-American attitude toward Italy, since it put an end to thoughts of military collaboration, even though it took several days before the extent of the disaster became clear. Both Roosevelt and Churchill had hoped for collaboration, and during the first Quebec Conference (August 11–24, 1943) they had modified the unconditional surrender policy with the "Quebec Memorandum." Churchill continued to express the greatest confidence in an Italian initiative, trying to bring the Foreign Office over to his views. In particular, in a September 7 letter he stated: "It seems to me that Italy has much to give.... The Italians have got to work their passage but if they make good we ought to treat them in everything but name, as allies. It may be they will fight much better with us than they ever did for Hitler."[61]

On September 9, Churchill, then in Washington, presented his views to Roosevelt and the American Joint Chiefs of Staff in an effort to persuade the Americans to seize the new opportunities opened by the armistice with Italy. Churchill's memorandum shows how extensive were the hopes arising from the Italian commitment to join the Allied side actively and the expectation that the battle for Naples and Rome would make the Germans retreat "to the lines of the Apennines or the Po."[62] According to Churchill:

> The public must be gradually led to realise what we and our Combined Staffs have so fully in mind, namely, the conversion of Italy into an active agent against Germany. Although we could not recognise Italy as an ally in the full sense, we have agreed she is to be allowed to work her passage, and that useful service against the enemy will not only be aided but recompensed. Should fighting break out between Italians and Germans, the public prejudices will very rapidly depart, and in a fortnight or so matters may be ripe, if we can so direct events, for an Italian declaration of war against Germany. The question of the Italian flag flying from Italian ships, and even some arrangement of Italians manning those vessels under British or American control, requires

consideration. The whole problem of handling and getting the utmost use out of the Italian Navy requires review now on a high level.

. . . On the over-all assumption of a decisive victory in the Naples area, we are, I presume, agreed to march northward up the Italian peninsula until we come up against the main German positions. If the Italians are everywhere favourable and their Army comes over to help, the deployment of at least a dozen Italian divisions will be of great advantage in holding the front across Italy and in permitting relief of Allied forces.[63]

This memorandum is clear proof of the different position Italy would have been in had it at least tried to react against the Germans. The British prime minister was not immediately aware of the severity of the disaster. In the following days he continued to hope for an Italian military reaction. While Roosevelt was leaving Washington for his estate in Hyde Park, Churchill participated in another meeting with the American Joint Chiefs of Staff to convince them to send more troops to the Mediterranean to facilitate taking control, together with the Italians, of the Dodecanese Islands. It is clear that for Churchill the Italian armistice made it possible to attack the Balkans, even though he did not bring up the topic specifically, in order to avoid stirring up American mistrust.

Churchill also had to fight a battle on the domestic front to persuade his own government, as reflected in an exchange of messages on this topic with London. In a detailed analysis of the situation, the British Chiefs of Staff Committee expressed strong reservations on the prime minister's views, stressing that "we should not get involved in any major campaign in the Balkans," and indicated its hesitation about employing "doubtful Allies like Italians in important positions in the front line."[64] In his reply, Churchill repeated: ". . . it is altogether premature to write off the Italian armed forces as useless or not worth-while. They might fight better for us than they ever did for Hitler." And on the Balkan issue, he maintained that "it would be folly not to exploit the highly favourable possibilities now offered to us," possibilities that could lead to a German withdrawal from the region.[65] In fact, the loss of the Balkans was then the main concern of the German High Command. Again on September 13, as he traveled to Halifax, Churchill wired General Wilson to insist on the capture of Rhodes "with Italian aid," but on the 14th the Italians surrendered and handed over the city and the port to the Germans.[66] On the other hand, in areas where Italian troops continued to resist, the promised aid did not come and the Germans took ferocious revenge, executing the soldiers after they had surrendered.

It took several days before the Allied Force Headquarters in Algiers understood the situation. On September 10, Eisenhower sent an appeal to Badoglio: "The whole future and honor of Italy depends on the part which [Italy's] armed forces are now prepared to play." Badoglio's reply is astounding: on September 11, when spontaneous resistance in some formations in several Italian cities was becoming sporadic and most of the troops had handed over their weapons to the Germans, he stated, "Since yesterday orders have been communicated to all armed forces to act vigorously against German aggression." And he continued, ". . . it is absolutely necessary now, General, that we coordinate our actions, as we are fighting the same adversary."[67] If there had ever been any doubts on the Allied side, this message made it clear that no orders had been issued to fight the Germans at the moment of the armistice and that, as late as the 11th, the orders were limited to mounting a defense against the Germans only in the case of a German attack.

During those days, Castellano, who had stayed in Algiers with a military task force that was to coordinate joint actions between Italian and Allied troops, tried to send Italian ships with reinforcements to Corfù and Cephalonia. During the next two weeks, however, all Italian suggestions for military collaboration and the use of Italian divisions were blocked. The reason was explained by Bedell Smith on his return from Malta, where the long armistice had been signed in the meantime. The failure to defend Rome, where six divisions faced two German ones, had caused the Allies to lose all confidence in the fighting spirit of the Italian units.

5. The Signing of the Long Armistice

In the days after the armistice was announced, the British Foreign Office put pressure on Eisenhower and Macmillan in Algiers to have the Badoglio government sign the long armistice as well.[68] As previously noted, when the armistice was signed, the "long" text, containing the political and economic provisions for the surrender, was set aside to avoid Italian reluctance to accept such punitive conditions. Now the Allies had to decide whether to force the signing of the version that had already been approved, modify it to make it less harsh and better adapted to the new circumstances or set it aside, at least for the moment.

Once again, disagreements among the Allied decision makers came to the fore. On one side, the Foreign Office and Churchill, and now the Soviets as well, were pressing for the signing of the text already agreed on, albeit with various degrees of determination. On the other, Roosevelt and the military in Algiers either regarded the imposition of a new document on the Italians as superfluous or at least were requesting softer terms. The solution adopted after a prolonged debate between Algiers, London, Washington and Moscow, which dragged on until the eve of the Malta meeting on September 29, was to insist on signing the clauses as originally drafted.

A military mission led by the Englishman Noel Mason-MacFarlane, which included political advisers Murphy and Macmillan, traveled to Brindisi on September 13 to make contact with Badoglio and the king and to assess the situation. On its return, the mission recommended to Eisenhower that he not require the long armistice to be signed and that he entrust the Italian government with the administration of all the liberated territory in exchange for the inclusion of anti-Fascist parties in the government. Eisenhower endorsed this request and sent it to the Allied governments on

September 18, along with a proposal to give Italy "co-belligerent status."[69] Churchill accepted the second part of the proposal, but observed that "it would make it much easier for us all if the instrument of surrender even though somewhat superseded could now be signed."[70] Meanwhile, the British prime minister informed Stalin of the British point of view in order to ensure Soviet support.

Roosevelt and Secretary of War Stimson took advantage of Eisenhower's request to set aside a text they regarded as entirely superfluous. They sent Eisenhower a new five-part directive on September 23 requesting him to "withhold long term Armistice provisions pending further instructions" and authorizing him to make recommendations "to lighten the provisions of the Military Armistice in order to enable the Italians, within the limit of their capacities, to wage war against Germany."[71] In this directive Roosevelt specified that the text had been "agreed upon by the Prime Minister and myself." The president also sent a copy of the message to Churchill as "commentary."[72]

Everything seemed decided, but there was a new twist. Macmillan, who had also favored postponing the signing of the long armistice, wrote Churchill that in his view Badoglio and the king would not balk at signing it.[73] This important information prompted Churchill to return to his previous decision. In two telegrams to Roosevelt of September 24 and 25, he insisted on his views, supporting his argument with the favorable response from Stalin of the 22nd to his earlier message.[74]

The Soviets did not fail to intervene in this complex situation. From the beginning, they had been informed of the negotiations and had taken a more intransigent position than the British on the armistice terms. In a message delivered to the American Embassy and dated September 25, Soviet Foreign Minister Molotov stated that it was "particularly necessary to expedite the signature with Italy of detailed armistice terms." Any changes in the provisions already ratified could take place only "with the agreement of the governments concerned."[75]

In the face of this unexpected resistance from his two allies, the American president gave in and ordered Eisenhower to sign the long armistice immediately. At the same time, Churchill, who initially had sought and obtained opinions from the Soviets in order to bolster his own, reacted indignantly to the message from Molotov, arguing in a letter to Roosevelt, ". . . we cannot be put in a position where our two Armies are doing all the fighting but the Russians have a veto and must be consulted upon any minor variation of the armistice terms."[76] This was not to be the last time the USSR tipped the balance when British and American policies diverged.

Badoglio and Eisenhower signed the long armistice on September 29 in a meeting at Malta. Badoglio had tried in an earlier meeting to protest not so much the harsh clauses, but the characterization of the Italian surrender as "unconditional." However, with the consent of the king, he agreed to sign the text, after Eisenhower committed himself to some formal modifications and agreed to withhold the document from publication. Eisenhower maintained this commitment in spite of various attempts by the Foreign Office to make it public. Throughout the war, the most important consideration in keeping the terms of the agreement secret was that public knowledge of such harsh conditions would have harmed the Allies' image in Italy and provoked resentment. The text of the long armistice was not published until November 1945.[77]

6. The Armistice with Italy: A Lost Opportunity

In the Italian campaign insufficient military forces employed by the Allies combined with the German decision to defend every piece of Italian territory rather than withdraw to the Alps led to a stalemate that delayed the Allied advance. Among the few who realized in what direction things were moving was Dick Crossman, who as political warfare executive at Allied Force Headquarters had followed the armistice issue from the beginning. As early as September 14 he wrote to his director in London, Bruce Lockhart, stating that not much more could be done in the Mediterranean theater: "It now looks as though the Italian campaign may well last for the duration of the war. It is clear that from December on the Mediterranean will be a secondary front and a rather routine one." He therefore asked to "go back to my real job on the main enemy."[78]

As soon as the emergency of the first days had passed, the Combined Chiefs of Staff rejected Eisenhower's pressing requests that ships allotted to India be assigned to the Mediterranean, because it would "be inappropriate to divert landing craft requested for an active theater of operations to make them available to another where the decision has not yet been made."[79] However, in spite of the obvious inadequacy of available resources, the Allied Supreme Command was slow to realize that the advance on Rome would take many months rather than a few weeks. Forecasts from Allied commanders continued to be unjustifiably optimistic and based on the assumption of a sudden collapse of the German Reich. In October, there was still widespread confidence that Rome would be taken in November.[80]

As already noted, the Italian problem was intertwined with the crucial question of the Balkans. The Germans had always considered control of the Balkans to be of primary importance. Immediately after the Italian surrender, they hastened to send reinforcements to replace the Italian divisions there and to resume control of the front, with massive air raids on the Italian garrisons.[81] From the very beginning, Churchill urged General Wilson, commander in chief for the Middle East, to intervene in the Dodecanese Islands. However, Wilson did not have the necessary ships or landing craft. Moreover, the Americans were not convinced of the strategic importance of the Aegean and refused to change the decision already made to limit operations in the Mediterranean.[82]

Early in October, Churchill sent an urgent request directly to Roosevelt that Wilson be assigned the forces necessary for retaking Rhodes. In this letter, after summarizing the military situation in the eastern Mediterranean, he first openly expressed his conviction of the strategic importance of the Balkans:

> . . . I believe it will be found that the Italian and Balkan Peninsulas are militarily and politically united and that really it is one theatre

with which we have to deal. It may indeed not be possible to conduct a successful Italian campaign ignoring what happens in the Aegean. The Germans evidently attach the utmost importance to this Eastern sphere and have not hesitated to divert a large part of their straitened air force to maintain themselves there. They have to apprehend desertion by Hungary and Roumania and a violent schism in Bulgaria. At any moment Turkey may lean her weight against them. We can all see how adverse to the enemy are the conditions in Greece and Yugoslavia. When we remember what brilliant results have followed from the political reactions in Italy induced by our military efforts should we not be shortsighted to ignore the possibility of a similar and even greater landslide in some or all of the countries I have mentioned? If we were able to provoke such reactions and profit by them our joint task in Italy would be greatly lightened.

... I have never wished to send an army into the Balkans but only agents' supplies and Commandos to stimulate the intense guerrilla [activity] prevailing there.... What I ask for is the capture of Rhodes and the other islands of the Dodecanese.[83]

Churchill's letter clearly reflects his belief that the Italian armistice had offered a golden opportunity to the Allies in the Balkans, which they were losing by their inaction.

Churchill's request met with Roosevelt's firm opposition to any diversion from the decisions made at the Quebec Conference to limit operations in the Mediterranean. Roosevelt's reply, prepared by his chief of staff, Admiral William D. Leahy, the connecting link between the president and the American Joint Chiefs of Staff, was a blunt and definitive no, since "no diversion of forces or equipment should prejudice overlord as planned."[84] Stimson expressed satisfaction with the resumption of a united American front after Roosevelt's concessions to Churchill during the previous months, commenting in his diary, "This will be a salutary lesson."[85] From then on, Churchill's appeals to Roosevelt for the necessary resources to win the race to Rome and avoid "sinking in Italy" and letting the situation "degenerate into a deadlock" fell on deaf ears.[86]

Disappointment at the unfulfilled hopes for the Italian campaign certainly contributed to the changed attitude of Roosevelt, who had previously accepted most of Churchill's suggestions. The liberation of Rome had been expected by October, but the Allies were only in Naples by then, and that with great effort. Roosevelt's attitude and that of his staff were therefore dictated not only by military opportunity, but also by the perception that Churchill was mainly interested in keeping the Mediterranean area and the Balkans in the British sphere of influence. Roosevelt was quite concerned about the prospect of maintaining troops in Yugoslavia, which would be equivalent to accepting a British sphere of influence in that area, supported by American military forces.

The events of the summer and fall of 1943 and the Soviet military victories of that period had an opposite effect on the British and on the Americans. For the British, the Soviet advance directly threatened an area regarded as essential to their sphere of influence, while the Americans concluded that a Soviet occupation of the Balkans and Central Europe was inevitable and argued in favor of their plan to push directly for Germany, a country over which they wanted to take control. This American position was obvious from the time of the first Quebec Conference and was expressed unequivocally in preparation for the Teheran Conference of November 1943.

The delay in operations and the lack of positive results on the Italian front made it increasingly urgent to settle on a strategic doctrine. At the Teheran Conference, the choice was left to Stalin. On his urging, the absolute priority of the strategy elaborated by the Americans and supported by the Soviets to open a second front in Normandy was reaffirmed and a date was set for the landing. Operations in Italy were conditional on the availability of spare forces. The Italian campaign was therefore continued with divisions sufficient to block the German forces in Italy, but not for an offensive that would force them into a definitive retreat. Consequently, the northern areas, the most industrialized and productive in Italy, were exploited until the end of the conflict by Germany and were freed only a week before the fall of Germany and the conquest of Berlin.

Conclusion

In this final chapter I will compare the objectives set by the parties involved in Italy's surrender with the results achieved, and consider in a historical context the consequences for Italian public sentiment and collective memory of the humiliating manner in which the surrender was carried out.

Beginning with the Allies, it must be pointed out that this study has devoted little space to the ideological aspects of Allied policy regarding Italy, since the Allies then ascribed scant importance to these aspects. The role of the Anglo-American governments is therefore described very differently here than in other historical writing. In most studies the guiding principle of Allied policy toward Italy is portrayed as anti-Communism, which is said to have influenced the British and American policy toward Italy after the surrender and to have gradually developed into an attempt to control if not "liquidate" the Resistance.[1] Italian discussion of this issue has been tainted for years by ideology. Some writers have argued this theory without considering the political objectives of the three great powers, the United States, Great Britain and the Soviet Union, or taking account of the complex military strategy of which the Italian campaign was only a part.

The development of Anglo-American policy toward Italy should be sufficiently clear from its reconstruction in these pages. The Allied objectives were obvious and definite, even if there were significant differences between the English and American governments. The common primary objective was to "eliminate Italy from the war," while adhering to the unconditional surrender principle and considering the German occupation of Italy as a likely result in the event of Italy's collapse. Italy's offer of military collaboration added a second, more ambitious objective to the first, that of a German withdrawal and the prompt liberation of Italy. Only the first of these was achieved. Would it have been possible to achieve the second as well?

The Allies' principal error was to underestimate the German response and to overestimate the Badoglio government's will and capacity to act against the Germans. All Allied evaluations took for granted that the Germans would withdraw at least to a position between Pisa and Rimini, if not to the Alps, and that Rome would remain under Italian control. The Allies did not seriously believe that the Germans, with Italy's defection, could simultaneously retain control of a good part of Italy and the Balkans, where they had to replace the Italian troops. Further, the Anglo-American leaders uncritically accepted the Badoglio government's declaration of "anti-Fascism" – that is, its opposition to the preceding regime – with no comprehension of the king's deep reluctance to disengage himself from the past or of the limitations his reluctance imposed on the viable options.

On the other hand, the Allies could not be accused of deceiving the Italians by allowing them to believe there would be a major landing or by not giving away their own strategy. They could in no way have divulged information on their planned landings to representatives of a country with which they were still at war. Badoglio himself declared that it would be naive to ask for it. The Allies could not rule out the possibility that the Italians were playing a double game or that the Germans would execute a coup. In both cases the Germans, if they had had knowledge of Allied plans, could have forced the Allies back into the sea and caused them grave losses. It was certainly an error not to warn the Italians that the date of the landing was imminent. On the other hand, Castellano, and especially Ambrosio, were foolish to infer a definite date from a confidential statement by Bedell Smith.

The Anglo-American governments and military commands cer-

Conclusion

tainly committed major errors of judgment during the improvised Italian campaign, which was characterized by increasingly open opposition by the American Chiefs of Staff and by the secretary of war, Stimson, concerned as they were over an excessively prolonged involvement in Italy. The Italian front was of secondary importance from the start, because the outcome of the war would have in fact been decided on the eastern front and later on in Normandy. However, the campaign did achieve its overt objective, that of taking Italy out of the war and tying up some German divisions, keeping them from the Russian front during the crucial period of the Red Army offensive at Kursk. Nevertheless, it remains doubtful whether the overall Allied strategy was correct and whether it was reasonable to open a front, even a marginal one, with such limited forces. With larger forces and coordination between the Mediterranean and Middle Eastern operations, which barely existed, the Germans might have been induced to withdraw from central Italy, permitting the Allies to keep control of those areas in the Balkans and the Aegean where considerable Italian forces were in fact deployed.

It may be argued that a more aggressive initial approach by the Anglo-American forces could have persuaded the Germans to withdraw, making possible the rapid advance everyone expected, a theory supported by German sources as well. But the landing at Salerno was nearly a disaster because of unexpected German resistance, and, even at the time, the cautious conduct of Eisenhower's and Alexander's operations was not free of criticism.

The Allied policy to relegate Italy to a position of secondary importance, combined with the Italian government's decision not to organize resistance and active collaboration with the Anglo-Americans, meant that the initiative on the Italian front passed to the Germans. Immediately after July 25, the German High Command had already considered leaving Italy and had prepared a line of defense in the Alps to which its troops were to withdraw. The divisions moving into Italy at that time remained at first in the north, in defense of the frontiers and in the expectation of an Anglo-American landing. The Germans' principal objective was to retain occupation of northern Italy, both to exploit Italian labor and industry and to prevent the Allied air bases from moving closer, which would have facilitated air raids on Germany and directly threatened the German presence in Yugoslavia. Only after the armistice was announced did the Germans decide to occupy central and southern Italy, after they became aware of the insufficiency of the Allied offensive forces and the passivity of the Italians. Thus both Allied and Italian hopes that the Germans would withdraw were deluded.

On the Italian side, the picture that emerges is one of total inaction and irresponsibility by the Badoglio government and the military leaders, and an overestimation of the importance of a beaten and prostrate Italy. This manifested itself, among other things, in absurd Italian claims to provide advice and to enlighten the Anglo-Americans, as if they were ignorant of their own interests.

After the war, all Italian political leaders and military commanders claimed both that they wanted to achieve an armistice with the Allies as soon as possible and that they believed that changing sides was necessary.[2] In reality, this "common desire" was not apparent in the days following Mussolini's dismissal. The armistice negotiations were conducted from the first with a great deal of uncertainty and in an atmosphere of mutual distrust within the military commands and the government. Although the Italians generally believed by then that the war was lost, they clung to the illusion that Italy could leave the war without direct conflict with the Germans, which everyone feared as the worst alternative.

The king and Badoglio could have decided to make public the German plans for a coup against the government and call the people and the armed forces to the nation's defense. If they had done so immediately after July 25, and closed the Brenner Pass to prevent the influx of German divisions, as the German command feared they would, occupation of at least part of the country could have been avoided. The decision to flee from Rome in order to escape capture would have been legitimate only if defenses against German aggression had been organized. But the king and Badoglio completely mistrusted the armed forces and their commanders, and were primarily concerned not with the good of the nation, but with their own personal safety. They feared that any popular reaction could set off a revolution. Regrettably, there was no Italian de Gaulle who could take the initiative or who had the authority to appeal for the defense of the threatened nation.

It is impossible to establish with any certainty what attitude prevailed at the upper levels of the military, but there clearly was a strong current of opinion against changing sides and in favor of continuing the German alliance. Various explanations for this attitude have been proposed: dread of assuming personal responsibility, fear of German reaction, ideological conviction and the sense of honoring an alliance.

On the other hand, only the king, who then represented the sole authority recognized by all political forces and by the armed forces, would have been able to lead Italy rapidly to the Anglo-American side. However, his personality, his indecisive character, his twenty-year association with Fascism (plus his share of responsibility for it) and his deep mistrust of the anti-Fascist forces all contributed to making an initiative on his part most improbable, unless strongly pressed by extraordinary circumstances. The king simply was not capable of meeting the tasks he faced. Thus no action was taken to change sides, and military preparations against the expected Allied landing continued to the end. This choice cannot be justified by "requirements of secrecy." Attempting to spare part of the country from German occupation, or at least mitigate the occupation with an offensive action, required taking a position against one's own past and running personal risks, which neither the king nor Badoglio had any intention of doing.

It is probable that the Badoglio government attempted to the end to maintain its option of taking the less risky course. The government acted with a complete lack of concern for the country's interests and with deep cynicism about the likely sacrifices of the army positioned outside Italy. All decisions were made officially by the king, even that of taking the three armed forces ministers with him on his flight from Rome. This absolved them from any further responsibility. However, while the decision to surround with the greatest secrecy both the negotiations under way and the signing of the armistice before September 8 may perhaps be justified by the need to let nothing leak to the Germans, the decision by the king, the Supreme Command and the Army General Staff not to implement the execution of Memoria 44 after the armistice announcement is incomprehensible and clearly unjustifiable. Still to be considered is the issue of the different kinds of behavior and the individual choices when the armistice was proclaimed. As I have noted, the Army and Navy General Staffs behaved quite differently. While the Navy General Staff continued to function even after the departure of de Courten, the headquarters of the Army General Staff, together with the War Ministry and the Supreme Command, were immediately abandoned by their senior officers. Requests for orders from peripheral units in Italy and abroad were not answered.

The total absence of action at the top immediately after the armistice announcement was interpreted as a decision at the highest level not to fight the Germans. Specifically, it was translated into the order of the day: "Let's all go home." However, the commanders and soldiers who continued to fight the Germans and who disobeyed orders to surrender their arms were far more numerous than has generally been thought. Their individual decisions must have been much more difficult to make than a decision simply to obey orders, all the more so because this meant opposing an ally of only a few hours before. These acts of resistance, though isolated, are of fundamental importance.

The refusal by the Badoglio government and the Supreme Command to order fighting the Germans, the numerous episodes of cowardice and the total acquiescence to the Germans constitute one of the saddest and most humiliating chapters in Italian history.

In the most sensational case, the failure to defend Rome, the decision was made almost immediately upon receipt of the first news of German offensive action despite the clear superiority of the Italian forces, which had been deployed and prepared for the very purpose of defending the government against a German coup. Decisive action on that occasion would have indicated a clear choice, whatever the final outcome, and would have had enormous consequences by demonstrating the unity of the Italian army and its willingness to participate with the Allies in the battle under way, leading to German withdrawal north of the capital and a more rapid liberation of the country. However, the Badoglio government made no specific choice either for Rome or for the rest of the country, deciding to do nothing while awaiting German actions. That the defense of Rome was not even brought up in the famous meeting of the Crown Council of September 9 is highly significant. The question of preparing for resistance was not even seriously considered and was left completely in Carboni's hands. An opinion taken from an Allied source is certainly correct:

> ... with a little prior organization what was certainly a difficult situation could have been managed in a way to reflect less discredit on the Italian nation in the eyes of the world.[3]

The events of September 1943 demonstrate that twenty years of totalitarianism had destroyed the capacity of the ruling class, especially the Italian military, to assume responsibility and make decisions. They also constitute clear proof of the monarch's inadequacy for the grave task of leading Italy out of and beyond the experience of Fascism.

Whatever judgment is made of the way Italy withdrew from the conflict, there was no alternative and the choice to disengage itself from Germany was of fundamental importance for Italy's future. The country emerged beaten from the war, but without the stain of having maintained the Fascist regime to the end. Acceptance of the surrender, even if unconditional, was the only course to take when the country was no longer in a position to fight; not to accept it would only have meant more death and greater destruction.

An issue that remains contested is whether it was legitimate for Italy to change sides and fight against its former ally. I refer to the accusation of treason leveled by Hitler and the Fascists of the Italian Social Republic against the government and the monarchy. Perhaps the king and the military commanders, themselves victims of the same strange logic, attempted to absolve themselves from this accusation when giving orders not to fire the first shot against the Germans. This question remains alive, though often unexpressed, among certain segments of the public. According to this view, Italy would have left the conflict with a better image had it fought to the end, because the actions taken on September 8 and in subsequent weeks were humiliating, diminished the nation's dignity and earned international contempt for Italy. This view considers the Italo-German alliance as a traditional one and completely ignores the fact that Italy had followed Nazi Germany into a war that increasingly meant imposition of a social order based on the supposed racial supremacy of the Germans, the extermination of the Jews and the destruction of entire nations. To continue to the end would have meant sharing Hitler's plans, as well as the destruction of a country that shared Germany's fate.

Many German officers believed that Italy would continue its alliance with Germany. When Kesselring heard that Italy had requested the armistice, he simply refused to believe it, "because for us Germans the defeat of a people is worse than death."[4]

For the Germans, the Italian signing of the armistice was itself a "betrayal," independent of a change of sides; thus Italy was immediately treated de facto as an enemy country. The German High Command immediately gave the order to execute Operation Achse. The attempts of the Italian commanders to avoid conflicts and not to take offensive action were therefore not only useless but counterproductive, since they only delivered Italy to the Germans and certainly did not preserve Italy's honor.

The accusation of "betrayal" distorts historical reality, even if we ignore the sort of alliance of which Italy was a part and even if we leave unconsidered the right of a nation to end a conflict to avoid total destruction after "having lost all capacity to resist," as Badoglio put it in the message sent to Hitler on the evening of September 8. Germany considered Italy a satellite country that was to serve German interests, not its own, even at the cost of occupying its territory and placing the whole government under arrest. We must ask ourselves not whether the Badoglio government acted correctly in deciding to surrender, but why so much precious time was lost. Italy did not react when the Germans violated its territorial integrity, and it procrastinated in abandoning the war until it was

Conclusion

an occupied country. On the other hand, the Germans repaid Badoglio's "loyalty" to a former ally, pushed to the point of not giving orders to attack the Germans, by disarming the Italian army and shooting those who dared to resist and disobey.

Once the Germans had ascertained how inadequate the Italian forces were to resist an offensive on their own territory, as reported by the Italian commanders and Mussolini himself, the Germans made plans to occupy the country and disarm the Italian army while Mussolini was still in power. They perfected them immediately after July 25, when the Badoglio government had not yet contacted the Anglo-Americans. These are the factors some German historians draw on to argue that it was not an Italian but a "German betrayal."

The choice made by the king to flee Rome without giving any orders at the time of the armistice and the lack of leadership demonstrated on that crucial occasion were probably decisive in the referendum of 1946, in which the vote prevailed against the monarchy. In 1943 the entire population of Italy paid for the collapse of governmental authority. The armed forces maintained their loyalty to the monarchy, as is shown by the soldiers interned in Germany who refused to abjure their oath to the king, but the population lost faith in the sovereign, which it had demonstrated in the days following July 25. By dismissing Mussolini, Victor Emmanuel III made people forget his association with Fascism, but national consensus and unity were shattered on September 8.

The choice of a clear break with the past, which the king had not been able to make, fell on the population as a whole. Most people adopted the "wait and see" attitude that had characterized the last years of the war, attempting to survive until the end of the conflict. Only a minority responded to the call from the reborn Fascist Party to "honor the fatherland" and show loyalty to the alliance with Germany, which by then was clearly occupying Italy.

September 8 also constituted an important turning point because the power vacuum caused by the collapse of a whole ruling class obliged part of the population to assess the disaster that the regime had inflicted on the country. In the days and weeks that followed, many Italians were forced to take sides, to choose between the two parties in the conflict. The leaders of the anti-Fascist opposition, who had accelerated the reorganization of their parties during the forty-five days between Mussolini's overthrow and the surrender, established the Committee of National Liberation on September 9 in Rome. But also many who had supported the Fascist regime until then decided to fight the German occupation and work for national renewal. These sentiments found their clearest expression in the Resistance movement.

The meaning of the tragedy of September 8 and the interpretation of the origins of the Resistance are issues that still divide historians as they divided Italians at the time. The internal conflict that characterized the postwar years in Italy prevented an objective reconstruction of the events of 1943. Up to now there has been no history of Italy for that period that is acceptable to all sides; there are only partial reconstructions, separate accounts with no common base: the story of the defeated and that of the victors. Most studies present an artificial contrast between two Italys, the Fascist one that died between July 25 and September 8 and the new one born on September 9 with the Committee of National Liberation and the Resistance. It is taken for granted that on September 8 and the days following, the army dissolved, and with it the previous state. The condemnation of the army, which disbanded ignominiously, is common to both the Fascists, who, like the Germans, looked on the armistice as a betrayal, and the anti-Fascists. According to Ugo La Malfa, then a leader of the Action Party, "Badoglio's great army existed and died in Italy on September 8."[5] Condemnation of the senior military and the government has been followed by condemnation of the army and the military in general: "There will never again be an army in Italy," Fenoglio has a soldier say in one of his stories, expressing the sense of emptiness and collapse he saw around him on September 8.[6]

This condemnation was issued by the emerging anti-Fascist ruling class, which considered September 8 and the fate of the army to be the final act of the preceding regime, while exalting the birth of the Resistance as the expression of a new Italy. Most historical studies follow this line of interpretation without ever verifying it.

Conclusion

In recent works, however, it has gradually been revised, in order to understand and explain with greater subtlety an extremely complex situation. In Claudio Pavone's book *Una guerra civile*, the choice in the days following the armistice between loyalty to the monarchy and loyalty to Mussolini is for the first time considered a legitimate "moral" one. Pavone, an intellectual of the Left, uses the concept of "civil war" to explain the struggle between partisans and exponents of the Italian Social Republic, thereby avoiding the usual condemnation of the followers of Mussolini voiced by historians of the Resistance.

The Italian republic emerging from the 1946 referendum was founded on the myths that the Resistance was a popular struggle and that the population adhered to the values of anti-Fascism. To support these myths it was necessary to deny the fact that the majority of the population had accepted the Fascist regime, thus upholding a false interpretation and preventing the country from coming to terms with its Fascist past.

In opposition to this historical version, recent studies stress the country's passivity when faced with the events of September 8 and the German occupation. Beyond the errors and faults of the ruling class and the military commanders, these observers see September 8 as the outcome of a deeper moral crisis in which Italy is still involved today.

It is certainly true that no Italian historian has felt the need to make an "examination of conscience" concerning the crisis of September 8 as Marc Bloch did in explaining the "strange defeat" of France in June 1940. However, historians like Bloch are rare not only in Italy but in France as well. After Bloch's death, for decades no other French historian engaged in a similar examination of conscience concerning the Vichy regime, as serious a phenomenon as September 8 for Italy. Only in recent years has the problem of Vichy France been presented as an issue that touches on the very morality of the nation.

The risk inherent in interpreting September 8 as "the autobiography of a nation" and a sign of a moral crisis of long duration, however, is that by pushing the origins of the crisis back in time, it becomes an alibi for the complete irresponsibility of the ruling class, thereby divesting the events associated with the Italian surrender of any concrete historical meaning.

September 8, in the collective memory and in the two opposing interpretations we have described, is regarded as that moment when the army dissolved and everyone decided to go home, the moment the Italian army was humiliated by surrendering its weapons to the Germans. It is a stigma that seems impossible to remove, an indelible sign of the Italian character. However, historians have never examined the actual behavior of the army, some viewing it as merely an instrument of the preceding regime, others as a reflection of the national crisis.

The reality is far more complex. The two Italys, that of September 8 and that of the Resistance, are much closer than has been apparent up to now. Many soldiers fleeing from their barracks could not reach their homes, and went into the mountains to join that minority of anti-Fascists who freely chose to fight the Germans. Moreover, many officers fought in partisan political formations. While in those days their significant role in the Resistance was recognized,[7] their lack of political motivation earned them a negative judgment in later historical studies. The unilateral interpretation of the Resistance as a revolutionary movement, given by the parties of the Left that took part in it, excluded all those who at the time of the armistice and over the next two years fought the Germans *exclusively* to defend the nation and uphold its honor. The "autonomous," namely nonpolitical, partisan formations were pejoratively labeled "badogliani" by those "resisters" whose motivation was political. When possible they were isolated, and in some areas there were also armed clashes.

The Resistance, however, was a repository for many different ideals and goals that defy any schematic or Manichaean interpretation.[8] The need to restore the nation's dignity, betrayed by Fascism and the Badoglio government, was indeed one of its dominant themes. The use of the term "patria" – fatherland – which did not then have the old-fashioned and almost pejorative tone that it later took on, was widespread among the partisans.

Conclusion

In historical studies, the patriotic element has been relegated to second place, while the concepts of the Resistance as a "civil" and a "class" war have prevailed – to borrow Claudio Pavone's most useful classification. Pavone's text is a good example of the contradictions that can be found in many histories of that period. It represents a turning point, since it introduces reflections on the patriotic theme, but at the same time it does not in the least free itself from old assumptions, dedicating to the patriotic war much less space than that devoted to the "civil" and "class" aspects of the conflict.

The idea of the Italian nation neither was destroyed by the trauma of September 8, nor ceased to represent an important reference point for both public life and personal identities during the Resistance. The fact that historical studies for so long ignored this aspect has more to say about the period in which they were written than about the period they were dealing with. It was after the establishment of post-Fascist democracy that the Italian national identity began to weaken; this was also a result of the political hegemony then achieved by the parties of the Left and the Catholic party, which received their legitimacy from supranational entities such as the USSR on the one side and the Vatican on the other. Furthermore, those parties had historically been forces of opposition to the Italian state, and did not share the ideals of the Risorgimento on which the nation had been built. When the need to mobilize public opinion in the immediate aftermath of the war had passed, the forces both of opposition and of government set aside the "national" element, which they had never really espoused. The anti-Fascist political parties that had fought in the Resistance became the building blocks of the new Italian republic; they gave it legitimacy and provided the Italians with means of expressing their political identity. The weakening of the idea of the nation, however, meant that a common ideological principle in which all Italians could recognize themselves was lacking. Partisan identities prevailed over and erased an Italian identity. Only in recent times has the emergence of the Northern League, a political force that sometimes advocates the dissolution of national unity, resulted both in a renewed interest in the origins of the process of denationalization and in an attempt to return to the certainties of yesterday.[9]

Perhaps the moment has come to rethink these issues in search of a unifying idea of the Italian past and to reconsider the establishment of the Italian republic beyond myths that are no longer valid. Such an effort must begin with the gulf brought on by September 8. The refusal of the post-Fascist political class and historians to settle accounts with historical events has artificially divided the nation into the old Italy of the collapse of the army and the new one of the anti-Fascist response. However, they are interconnected and the point where they intersect is represented by the chaotic period that followed the armistice.

Notes

Introduction

1. Several general histories of the period barely mention September 8, 1943, or omit it entirely as they pass from the events of the war to those of the Resistance. Two examples of this omission are Giampiero Carocci, *Storia d'Italia dall'unità ad oggi* (Milan, 1975), and Stuart Woolf, ed., *Italia, 1943–1950* (Bari, 1974).

2. For Allied intervention, see the telegram dated September 3, 1944, from Ellery Stone, head of the Allied Commission, to General Henry M. Wilson, Supreme Commander of the Allied forces in the Mediterranean, and information from Noel Charles to the British Foreign Office; and a second telegram from Charles to the Foreign Office dated September 13, 1944: FO 371/43874, Public Record Office (henceforth PRO), London. Allied pressure led Bonomi to attempt to suspend the inquiry. See Bonomi's correspondence with the War minister in the Archivio Centrale dello Stato, Rome, Casati papers, b. 3.

3. Mario Palermo, *Memorie di un comunista napoletano* (Parma, 1975), p. 284. The investigation was conducted "with much difficulty amid a conspiracy of silence [omertà], suspicion, reticence, and fear" (ibid. p. 285).

4. For the purge proceedings that opened in November 1944 against ten generals – among them Vittorio Ambrosio, Mario Roatta, Giacomo Carboni and Giuseppe De Stefanis – and for the failure to defend Rome, see Archivio dell'Ufficio Storico dello Stato Maggiore dell'Esercito (Archives of the Historical Office of the Army General Staff henceforth AUSSME) L13, fasc. 27, sottofasc. "Mario Roatta." On the attempt to indict Badoglio, see Elena Aga-Rossi, *L'Italia nella sconfitta* (Naples, 1985), pp. 141–42. The British housed Badoglio in their embassy in Rome until the Italian government guaranteed that the

proceedings would be halted, while the Americans preferred not to intervene.

5. On the guidelines followed by the military commission and on its inquiries, see AUSSME, L13, fasc. 24–33.

6. See "L'armistizio e la difesa di Roma nella sentenza del Tribunale militare," in *Rivista Penale* (May–June 1949), pp. 3–116.

7. The memoirs of Marshal Pietro Badoglio, *La seconda guerra mondiale* (Milan, 1946), and of General Giacomo Carboni, *L'armistizio e la difesa di Roma* (Rome, 1945), are completely unreliable. Carboni in particular even credits himself with the defense of Rome "protracted to the last limit of the possible and useful, against forces of preponderant power" (p. 17). Marred by omissions and ambiguity but useful in certain respects are those of General Francesco Rossi, *Come arrivammo all'armistizio* (Milan, 1946), and General Mario Roatta, *Otto milioni di baionette* (Milan, 1946). The memoirs of General Giuseppe Castellano, *Come firmai l'armistizio di Cassibile* (Milan, 1945), constituted the most important source on the armistice negotiations for many years. These memoirs trace the talks with the Anglo-Americans rather faithfully, but are entirely inadequate concerning the Italian domestic situation. Castellano's book ascribes to the military, and especially to Castellano himself, the initiative that led to Mussolini's fall, undervaluing the work of Dino Grandi and other Fascist leaders. Castellano also published *La guerra continua* (Milan, 1963). On the negotiations with the Anglo-Americans and the actions of the Army General Staff, see also Giacomo Zanussi, *Guerra e catastrofe d'Italia, giugno 1943–maggio 1945* (Rome, 1946).

8. The most significant case concerns the file of correspondence with the Anglo-Americans on the armistice negotiations and the documents in the Ufficio Operazioni Esercito relative to orders to military commands. They were destroyed on the morning of September 9, 1943, for fear that they would fall into German hands. A list of documents destroyed – which in some cases is the only evidence that a document existed – is in AUSSME and has recently been published in Ministero degli Affari Esteri, *I documenti diplomatici Italiani* (Italian diplomatic documents), 9th ser.: 1939–1943, vol. 10: February 7 to September 8, 1943 (Rome, 1990) (henceforth *DDI, 9/X*), pp. 957–58. Also burned on September 7 were the documents of the SIM (Italian Military Intelligence) (testimony of Infantry Warrant Officer Giovanni De Martis of July 18, 1944, in AUSSME, *Historical Diary, Castellano*, cart. 3000). On the other hand, documents are sometimes to be found in the files of the Army Historical Office despite a specific order from the Italian Supreme Command to destroy them. Guariglia, foreign minis-

ter at that time, also writes that he burned all the documents that could fall "either in the hands of the Germans or the Allies" (Raffaele Guariglia, *Ricordi, 1922–1946* [Naples, 1950], p. 676). At the time of his flight, Badoglio did not even take the text of the armistice with him. He requested a copy from the Allied military mission that came to Brindisi on September 13, arguing that he had never seen the armistice conditions.

9. Among the first group of authors is Ruggero Zangrandi, *1943: 25 luglio–8 settembre* (Milan, 1964) and *L'Italia tradita* (Milan, 1971). His critics have concentrated on the unsupported thesis that there was a secret agreement between Kesselring and Badoglio on the basis of which the Germans would have allowed the king and members of the Italian command to flee undisturbed in exchange for the surrender of Rome. This diminishes the value of the voluminous documentation Zangrandi assembled on the responsibilities of the military commands, the king and Badoglio for the disaster of September 8. Also in this first group are Emilio Lussu, *La difesa di Roma* (Sassari, Sardinia, 1987); and Ivan Palermo, *Storia di un armistizio* (Milan, 1967), fundamental because be publishes a selection from the interrogations by the commission his father chaired. Among the second group are Vanna Vailati, *L'armistizio e il regno del sud* (Milan, 1969) and *Badoglio racconta* (Turin, 1956); Massimo Mazzetti, "L'armistizio con l' Italia in base alle relazioni ufficiali angloamericane," in *Memorie storiche militari* (Rome, 1978). For a brief but accurate interpretive synthesis, see Denis Mack Smith, "The Italian Armistice of 1943," in *Malta: A Case Study in International Cross-Currents*, Stanley Fiorini and Victor Mallia Milanes (eds.) (Malta, 1991), pp. 253–66.

10. This documentation was first used in the mid-1960s in the volume by Albert Garland and Howard McGaw Smyth on the landing in Sicily and the Italian surrender, *Sicily and the Surrender of Italy*, which after many years is still the most complete study on the armistice and the Allies. Immediately afterward, Mario Toscano used this documentation for his volume, *Dal 25 luglio all' 8 settembre*, which originated as a comparison between the Italian sources and the revelations published in two official volumes by the U.S. government: the part on Italy in the volume *Foreign Relations* on Europe for 1943 (U.S. Department of State, *Foreign Relations of the United States* [henceforth *FRUS*], *1943*, vol. 2: *Europe* [Washington, D.C., 1964]), and in the work by Garland and McGaw Smyth. In subsequent years, the British and U.S. governments published several other useful studies for a reconstruction of the negotiations leading to the armistice. For the U.S. part, the most important publications are *FRUS: The Conferences at Washington and*

Quebec (Washington, D.C., 1970) and D. Eisenhower's correspondence in *The Papers of Dwight David Eisenhower: The War Years*, A. Chandler (ed.), vols. 2–3 (Baltimore, 1970); for the British part, L. Woodward, *British Foreign Policy in the Second World War*, vol. 2 (London, 1971), which contains a chapter on the Italian surrender, and M. Howard, *Grand Strategy, August 1942–September 1943*, vol. 4 (London, 1972). The view of the American military command is described in Robert J. Quinlan, "The Italian Armistice," in *American Civil-Military Decisions*, ed. Harold Stein (Birmingham, Ala., 1962), pp. 205–307.

11. Robert Murphy, *Diplomat Among Warriors* (New York, 1964); Harold Macmillan, *The Blast of War* (London, 1967); Kenneth Strong, *Intelligence at the Top: The Recollections of an Intelligence Officer* (London, 1968), pp. 100–53; David Dilks (ed.), *The Diaries of Sir Alexander Cadogan* (London, 1971); Harold Macmillan, *War Diaries: Politics and War in the Mediterranean* (New York, 1984); Kenneth Young (ed.), *The Diaries of Sir Robert Bruce Lockhart, 1939–1965*, 2 vols. (London, 1980).

12. The most relevant example is the presumed moving forward of the date of landing at Salerno and therefore of the announcement of the armistice. However, the whole question of relations with the Anglo-Americans has been incorrectly interpreted. Thus it was written that the Allies had never thought of sending an airborne division and had decided to cancel the operation without informing the Italians. It has also been argued that Alexander, convinced that the Italian army "would be wiped out," did not consider the possibility of its active involvement, before the armistice, in Allied operations. See Mazzetti, *L'armistizio con l'Italia*, p. 136, Pietro Secchia and Filippo Frassati, *Storia della resistenza. La guerra di liberazione in Italia, 1943–1945*, 2 vols. (Rome, 1965), vol. 1, pp. 70–72, 80–83; Ennio Di Nolfo, *Le paure e le speranze degli italiani (1943–1945)* (Milan, 1986), p. 48; Vailati, *L'armistizio e il regno del sud*, pp. 226–31.

13. In general, works on the history of the Italian Resistance hardly mention the resistance against the Germans offered by the Italian regular troops in Italy and abroad. For a rare exception see Roberto Battaglia's classic *Storia della resistenza italiana* (Turin, 1964), pp. 76ff. The official report by the Historical Office, *Le operazioni delle unità italiane nel settembre–ottobre 1943*, compiled by Mario Torsiello (Rome, 1975), though inaccurate in several places, gives a detailed account of those events and offers a very dry listing, placing cowardly and heroic acts on the same level; see also by Torsiello, *Settembre 1943* (Milan, 1963). Very useful is Gerhard Schreiber, *Die italienischen Militärinternienten im*

deutschen Machbereich, 1943–1945 (Munich, 1990), based on German military archives. References are to the Italian translation: *I militari italiani internati nei campi diconcentrazione del Terzo Reich, 1943–1945* (Rome, 1992); see also Domenico Bartoli, *L'Italia si arrende* (Milan, 1983); Filippo Stefani, *8 settembre 1943. Gli armistizi dell'Italia* (Settimo Milanese, 1991). See also the proceedings of the conferences: *8 settembre. Lo sfacelo della quarta armata* (Turin, 1979) and *8 settembre 1943. L'armistizio italiano 40 anni dopo* (Rome, 1985). Surprisingly little space is devoted to this topic by Lutz Kinkhammer, *L'occupazione tedesca in Italia* (Torino, 1993), who repeats the traditional judgment, that "in a few days Italian armies completely disintegrated" (p. 32).

14. For these data see Giorgio Rochat, "La resistenza militare nell'eloquenza dei numeri," in *Storia e Memoria*, no. 2 (1996), pp. 57–69.

Chapter One

1. Churchill to Roosevelt, July 25, 1941, in *Churchill and Roosevelt: The Complete Correspondence*, Warren F. Kimball (ed.), vol. 1 (Princeton, N.J., 1984), p. 224.

2. See David Dilks (ed.), *Retreat from Power: Studies in Britain's Foreign Policy of the Twentieth Century*, vol. 2 (London, 1981), p. 7; Michael E. Howard, *The Mediterranean Strategy in the Second World War* (London, 1968), pp. 7–8.

3. The phrase is that of Sir Percy Loraine, British ambassador in Rome in 1939–40. It is found in his memorandum to the Chiefs of the British General Staff of September 21, 1940, cited in a long document (164 typewritten pages, including notes) entitled *The Italian Armistice*, in CAB 101/144, PRO. The phrase is on pp. 87–88. The document was published in an Italian translation of sources I edited (E. Aga-Rossi, *L'inganno reciproco. L'armistizio tra Italia e gli anglo-americani del settembre, 1943* (Rome, 1993). The long document will be cited henceforth as *The Italian Armistice*, with page citations from both the original document and the Italian translation.

4. See the reports of the Joint Planning Staff, "Future Strategy," of August 21, 1940, and "Future Plan No. 1," of November 14, 1940, cited in *The Italian Armistice*. On the position of the British government and the intelligence services during the first years of the war, see Frederick W. Deakin, "Lo Special Operations Executive e la lotta partigiana," in *L'Italia nella seconda guerra mondiale e nella resistenza*, F. Ferratini Tosi, G. Grassi and M. Legnani (eds.) (Milan, 1988), pp. 99ff.

5. In December 1940, the British government requested the mediation of

the Holy See in order to establish a separate peace with Italy on the basis of agreements between Italy and England in 1938. There were two distinct démarches, one to the apostolic delegate in Sofia and the other to the apostolic delegate in London. However, the Vatican made no reply. See *Actes et documents du Saint Siège relatifs à la Seconde guerre mondiale*, vol. 4 (Vatican City, 1967), docs. 206 and 239. On this topic see Aga-Rossi, *L'Italia nella sconfitta*, p. 61.

6. See "Memorandum on the Use of Italian Prisoners of War for Anti-Fascist Political Work," FO 371/29936, PRO, in Aga-Rossi, *L'inganno*, pp. 237–42.

7. Concerning these activities, see the interesting work of Richard Lamb, *The Ghosts of Peace* (Salisbury, 1987), p. 147, which points out that not only did Eden and Churchill not mention them in their auto-biographies, but also Sir Llewellyn Woodward, the official historian of British foreign policy during World War II, fails to mention them. I thank Sir Frederick Deakin for giving me copies of some British foreign policy documents from that period from the Public Record Office, which he cited in his essay. See the documents published in Section 2 of Aga-Rossi, *L'inganno*. On British agents parachuting into Italy, see De Felice, *Mussolini l'alleato*, p. 811, and Ben Pimlott, *The War Diaries of H. Dalton* (London, 1986).

8. For the text of the speech, see *Winston Churchill: His Complete Speeches, 1897–1963*, Robert R. James (ed.), vol. 6 (New York, 1974), pp. 6322–25.

9. Churchill to Ismay, February 11, 1941, FO/371 29925, PRO. See Aga-Rossi, *L'inganno*, pp. 242–43.

10. See Anthony Eden, *The Reckoning* (Boston, 1965), p. 350.

11. The expression "sinking or surviving" is found in a memorandum by Eden of February 17, 1942, *Avon Papers*, FO 954/13, PRO. For Samuel Hoare's position, see his conversation with K. Skorzewski of September 1941 (ibid.), confirmed by his accommodating attitude even later, i.e., when he met Castellano in Madrid. Hoare's attitude contrasts with the rigid view of British ambassador Campbell in Lisbon.

12. In his memoirs, Eden reports a widespread view among British military officers that the Italian forces in Africa would be "easy prey" for the British as soon as the latter took the offensive. See Eden, *The Reckoning*, p. 184. On Eden's attitude toward Italy, due perhaps to his difficult relations with the Fascist regime, see the testimony of Cadogan in *The Diaries of Sir Alexander Cadogan*, entry for August 11, 1943.

13. On U.S. openness to Italy in 1940–42, see the testimony of Secretary of State Cordell Hull in his *Memoirs of Peace and War*, vol. 2 (New York, 1948), pp. 1558ff., and the message from the State Department

transmitted to the Italian ambassador to Washington, the prince
Ascanio Colonna di Paliano, on his return to Italy, stating that in the
United States there was "no extended resentment against Italy as
compared with the resentment against Germany and Japan" and when
"the time comes for Italy to make her own decisions the Italian people
may count on a sympathetic hearing in this country." Cited in Ennio
Di Nolfo, "Italia e Stati Uniti. Un'alleanza diseguale," *Storia delle
relazioni internazionali* 6 (1990–91), pp. 3ff. See also the notes of
Monsignor Domenico Tardini, secretary of the Congregation of Extraordinary Ecclesiastical Affairs, of June 8–9, 1943, enclosing the "plans
for oral and confidential communication of the nuncio to His Majesty,"
on requests from the U.S. government through Myron Taylor, Roosevelt's personal representative at the Vatican, for a separate peace with
Italy. See *Actes et Documents*, vol. 7, pp. 414–15. During the war, the
Vatican became a privileged interlocutor of the United States, but the
hierarchy was reluctant to become involved for fear of possible German
reprisals.

14. FO 371/33240, by Frederick W. Deakin, *Lo Special Operations
Executive*, p. 100. On the Lussu–Gentili contacts, see A. Varsori,
"L'antifascismo e gli alleati. Le missioni di Lussu e Gentili a Londra
e Washington nel 1941," *Storia e Politica* 19, no. 3 (1980), pp.
457–507.
15. *The Italian Armistice*, p. 12, in Aga-Rossi, *L'inganno*, pp. 97–98.
16. *Department of State Bulletin*, November 14, 1942.
17. *New York Times*, November 15, 1942, p. 12.
18. *The Italian Armistice*, p. 14, in Aga-Rossi, *L'Inganno*, pp. 99–100. Cf.
Llewellyn Woodward, *British Foreign Policy*, vol. 5 (London, 1976), pp.
462–63; Aga-Rossi, *L'Italia nella sconfitta*, pp. 74ff.
19. The text of the memorandum can be found in Winston Churchill,
The Second World War, vol. 5 *Closing the Ring* (Boston, 1951), pp.
53–55.
20. Minute of Eden to the prime minister, December 2, 1942, in *The Italian
Armistice*, pp. 20–21, in E. Aga-Rossi, *L'inganno*, p. 106. According to
Varsori, it was instead Eden's rigid moralism that led him to reject emissaries from Fascist circles. See Antonio Varsori, "Italy, Britain and the
Problem of Separate Peace during the Second World War: 1940–43,"
Journal of Italian History, 1, no. 3 (Winter, 1978), p. 470.
21. Meeting of the War Cabinet of December 3, 1942, in *The Italian
Armistice*, pp. 18–19, in Aga-Rossi, *L'inganno*, pp. 103–5.
22 *The Diaries of Sir Robert Bruce Lockhart*, vol. 1, p. 209.
23. François Darlan was chief of the French Naval General Staff from 1939
and foreign minister in the Pétain government in February 1941.

Although a supporter of collaboration with Germany, he made an abrupt about-face in November 1942 and concluded an agreement with the American commander just before the Allied landing in North Africa, to prevent French resistance against the Allied troops. The British and American public harshly criticized the decision to use, for military expediency, a figure so closely tied to the Germans. Darlan was assassinated in December 1942 in Algiers.

24. Robert Sherwood, *Roosevelt and Hopkins: An Intimate History*, rev. ed. (New York, 1950), pp. 108, 124–27. There is a slightly different account in Elliott Roosevelt, *As He Saw It* (New York, 1946), p. 117.

25. FRUS, *The Conferences at Washington, 1941–42, and Casablanca, 1943* (Washington, D.C., 1972), p. 506. See also Harley Notter, *Postwar Foreign Policy Preparation, 1939–45* (Washington, D.C., 1949), p. 127, and Herbert Feis, *Churchill-Roosevelt-Stalin: The War They Waged and the Peace They Sought* (Princeton, N.J., 1957), p. 108. Note the contrast between the terms *unconditional surrender* and *armistice*.

26. See Hull, *Memoirs*, p. 1570. The secretary of state wrote incorrectly, "Originally, this principle had not formed part of the State Department's thinking" (ibid.).

27. This document is found in MR34/Italy, Sec. 1, Surrender of Italy, Franklin Delano Roosevelt Library (henceforth FDRL), and is published in Aga-Rossi, *L'inganno*, pp. 244–50.

28. *Principles Relating to the Military Occupation of Italy*, November 11, 1942, S Document 47, Policy Summaries, box 62, Notter Files, RG 59, National Archives and Records Service (henceforth NA).

29. Albert Wedemeyer, *Wedemeyer Reports!* (New York, 1958), pp. 185–86.

30. Winston Churchill, *The Second World War*, vol. 4, *The Hinge of Fate* (Boston, 1950), pp 683–86. WM 12th Conclusions, 20 January 1943, PREM 3/197/2, PRO; Sherwood, *Roosevelt and Hopkins*, p. 973.

31. *The Public Papers and Addresses of Franklin D. Roosevelt*, vols. 11 and 12 (New York, 1969). Roosevelt even suggested calling the Casablanca Conference the "unconditional surrender meeting." See Lord Hankey, *Politics: Trials and Errors* (Chicago, 1950), p. 29.

32. Sherwood, *Roosevelt and Hopkins*, p. 696.

33. Anne Armstrong, *Unconditional Surrender: The Impact of the Casablanca Policy upon World War II* (New Brunswick, N.J., 1961), p. ix. There is an extensive literature on the issue of unconditional surrender and its consequences. See also Paul Kecskemeti, *Strategic Surrender: The Politics of Victory and Defeat* (New York, 1964); A. E. Campbell, "Franklin Roosevelt and Unconditional Surrender," in *Diplomacy and Intelligence during the Second World War: Essays in*

Honour of F. H. Hinsley (Cambridge, 1985); R. G. O'Connor, *Diplomacy for Victory: FDR and Unconditional Surrender* (New York, 1971); N. S. Lebedeva, *Bezogovorocnaya kapitulyatsiya agressorov* [Unconditional surrender of the aggressors] (Moscow, 1988).

34. The text can be found in *War Messages of Franklin D. Roosevelt: December 8, 1941, to April 13, 1945* (Washington, D.C., 1950), p. 145.

35. Among the first to stress this aspect was William Langer in his essay "Political Problems of Coalition," *Foreign Affairs* (October 1947), p. 84.

36. Roosevelt brought up this point in a press conference on his return to Washington from Casablanca. See Feis, *Churchill–Roosevelt–Stalin*, p. 113.

37. Hanson Baldwin, *Great Mistakes of the War* (New York, 1950), p. 11. See also Wedemeyer, *Wedemeyer Reports!* p. 92.

38. See Gerhard L. Weinberg, *A World at Arms* (New York, 1994), pp. 609–11, and the documents in the British and American archives cited in the notes to these pages.

39. On the attempts to reach an agreement during the interval from July to October 1941, the most critical moment of the German invasion, see the article by the historian Dmitri Volkogonov in *Izvestya* of May 8, 1993, p. 5, and the revelations to the historian Lev Bezymensky by the diplomat Vladimir Seménov, who worked during the war at the Soviet Embassy in Stockholm and had a role in these contacts in the period 1941–42 (L. Bezymensky, "Sobralsia li Stalin Kapitulirovat' v 1941 godu?" [Did Stalin intend to surrender in 1941?], *Novoe Vremya*, 13 [1992], pp. 46–48). Among previous Western studies, see Peter Kleist, *Zwischen Hitler und Stalin, 1939–45* (Bonn, 1950); Alexander Fischer, *Sowjetische Deutschlandpolitik im zweiten Weltkrieg, 1941–45* (Stuttgart, 1975); Vojtech Mastny, *Russia's Road to the Cold War: Diplomacy, Warfare, and the Politics of Communism, 1941–45* (New York, 1979), pp. 73–85; H. W. Koch, "The Spectre of a Separate Peace in the East, Russo-German 'Peace Feelers," *Journal of Contemporary History* 10 (1975), pp. 531–47; I. Fleischauer, *Die Chance des Sonderfriedens. Deutsch–Sowjetische Geheimgespräche, 1941–45* (Berlin, 1986).

40. Stalin's speech was published in *Pravda* on May 1, 1943. Armstrong's opinion that "the Soviet Marshal . . . refused to adhere to the Unconditional Surrender doctrine until the final months of the war when he allowed the phrase to be included in the Yalta declaration" is wrong. On the Soviet attitude toward unconditional surrender, see Lebedeva, *Bezogovorochnaya kapitulyatsiya agressorov*, p. 87.

41. Stalin's expression, reported by Eden, was also mentioned by Churchill in a letter to Roosevelt of January 2, 1944; see *Churchill and Roosevelt: The Complete Correspondence*, vol. 2, *The Alliance Forged (November 1942–February 1944)*, Warren F. Kimball (ed.) (Princeton, N.J., 1984), p. 646. See the account of the conversation between Stalin, Roosevelt and Churchill of November 28, 1943, in FRUS, *The Conferences at Cairo and Teheran* (Washington, D.C., 1961), pp. 513–14. Churchill later recalled Stalin's position in January 1944. Roosevelt had completely forgotten it. See the prime minister's letter to Roosevelt of January 2, 1944, Roosevelt's answer of January 6 and the comments of the Foreign Office in PREM 3/197/2. The letters cited here are published in *Churchill and Roosevelt*, vol. 2, pp. 645–46 and 652.

42. Sherwood, *Roosevelt and Hopkins*, p. 697.

43. The document is published in part in ibid., pp. 721–24. The portion quoted is on p. 724.

44. John Wheeler-Bennett, "On the Making of the Peace" (typescript, p. 12), with comments by senior Foreign Office officials and a covering letter by Campbell, of the British Embassy in Washington to Gladwin Jebb of May 31, 1943 (FO 371/3519, PRO).

45. Kecskemeti, *Strategic Surrender*, p. 236.

46. Memorandum of conversation with President Roosevelt, September 9, 1944, Robert Murphy Papers, box 52/22, Hoover Archives, Stanford, Calif.

47. The English draft with thirty-nine articles is published in *The Italian Armistice*, pp. 51–55, and in Aga-Rossi, *L'inganno*, pp. 135–39.

48. See the American counterproposal in CAB 88 12, PRO, in Aga-Rossi, *L'inganno*, pp. 263–72.

49. The document, approved by the American Joint Chiefs of Staff and by Roosevelt in January 1944, was published in *Churchill and Roosevelt*, vol. 2, pp. 767ff. On the American position, see Keckskemeti, *Strategic Surrender*, p. 236. However, Keckskemeti did not have access to the documents now available.

50. Dispatch of Gladwin Jebb (in the name of the secretary of state) to Viscount Halifax, British ambassador in Washington, June 19, 1943, in FO371/35319, PRO, London.

51. *The Italian Armistice*, p. 58, in Aga-Rossi, *L'inganno*, p. 142.

52. Ibid.

53. *The Italian Armistice*, p. 61, in Aga-Rossi, *L'inganno*, p. 144.

54. See "Surrender Terms for Italy and Draft Declaration and Proclamation," June 16, 1943, in CAB 88/12, PRO, published in Aga-Rossi, *L'inganno*, pp. 251–63. For a discussion of the use of the term

"armistice" see the Foreign Office minutes "Use of Alternative Terms
for Armistice," June 3, 1943, FO 371/35319, PRO.

55. Several studies of these early feelers have been published and a great
deal of unpublished material can be found in the British archives. In
addition to Toscano's book and Varsori's *Italy, Britain*, the research of
Renzo De Felice has enriched the picture of these approaches. De Felice's
results were first published in his introduction to Dino Grandi's book
25 luglio. Quarant'anni dopo (Bologna, 1983) and later in the volume
Mussolini l'alleato, pp. 1155ff., to which the reader is referred for a
detailed analysis of the various positions taken in the months and days
preceding Mussolini's overthrow on July 25, 1943. An essential source
for British views on the Italian overtures is *The Italian Armistice*. See
also Lamb, *The Ghosts of Peace*, pp. 170ff.

56. This was an offer made by the brother of the American ambassador
in London, Clinton Winant, to the Italian consul in Lausanne, Gian
Gerolamo Chiavari, to act as intermediary with the government in
Washington. The offer, which Chiavari transmitted on August 5, 1943,
to Babuscio Rizzo, who had just been nominated chargé d'affaires to
the Vatican, was first considered and then allowed to lapse "after the
first approaches," on August 29. See *DDI/9*, X, docs. 608, 646, 700
and 728.

57. See *The Italian Armistice*, p. 23, in Aga-Rossi, *L'inganno*, p. 108.

58. Salazar talked on July 23 with Sir Ronald Campbell, the British ambassador in Lisbon, to whom the other Italian emissaries had also
turned, maintaining that it would be far preferable to have a central
government with which relations could be established than a country
in ruin and chaos. Campbell limited himself to repeating that the
premise for any contact must be complete surrender. See Campbell's
report on the conversation with Salazar in *Avon Papers*, FO 954/13,
PRO.

59. This description is in *Actes et Documents*, vol. 7, p. 415. On the attitude of Victor Emmanuel III, see Denis Mack Smith, *Italy and Its
Monarchy* (New Haven, Conn., 1989), pp. 300–1.

60. See Grandi's account of the conversation, in which for the first time
Victor Emmanuel III let it be understood that he would take action, but
without being more explicit. The king took leave of Grandi with the
statement "Trust your king." See Dino Grandi, "Pagine di diario del
1943," *Storia contemporanea*, 14, no. 6 (1983), pp. 1059–60.

61. On the king's attitude toward the Anglo-Americans, see Paolo Puntoni,
Parla Vittorio Emanuele III (Bologna, 1993), pp. 133 and 188. An
attempt by Myron Taylor, Roosevelt's personal representative to the

Vatican, to discern the king's intentions, using Vatican intervention, had negative results. See *Actes et Documents*, vol. 7, pp. 414ff.

62. See the conversation between Leonardo Vitetti, director general for European and Mediterranean affairs at the Foreign Ministry, and the duke d'Acquarone on June 9, in *DDI/9*, X, pp. 527ff. Vitetti tried on that occasion to warn Acquarone against excessive optimism, emphasizing Badoglio's incompetence. In Vitetti's view, Badoglio would be unable to "master so complicated and dangerous a situation."

63. This was Vitetti's opinion, as emerges from the cited conversation with Acquarone.

64. Cited in J. Lukacs, *The Great Powers and Eastern Europe* (New York, 1953), p. 501.

65. See the account of the Mussolini–Hidaka conversation of July 25, 1943, at 12 PM in *DDI/9*, X, pp. 711–12, and Mussolini's correspondence with Hitler, especially Mussolini's letters of March 8 and 26, 1943, in *Hitler e Mussolini. Lettere e documenti* (Milan, 1946), and now in *DDI/9*, X, pp. 128–32 and 199–200. On the decisive influence of this idea on Mussolini's policies, see De Felice, *Mussolini l'alleato*, passim. The account of the conversation is on pp. 1387ff. Mussolini returned to the topic even after his fall. The testimony of Admiral Franco Maugeri is interesting. Maugeri was ordered to bring Mussolini to the island of Ponza and later recorded Mussolini's long outburst in *Mussolini mi ha detto* (Rome, 1944), pp. 25ff. Rumors of German–Soviet contacts continued to circulate in the following weeks, though they were always denied. Castellano reported them to the Anglo-Americans. See *DDI/9*, X, docs. 598, 673, 686, 723, 738, 749, 763, and Aga-Rossi, *L'inganno*, doc. 8.4, p. 400.

66. Giuseppe Bastianini, *Uomini, cose, fatti. Memorie di un ambasciatore* (Milan, 1959). Bastianini requested a Vatican passport for one Fummi, a banker who represented American financial interests in Europe and who was to establish contacts with the Allies (pp. 115–17). On Bastianini's actions and the position of various participants in July 25, see De Felice, *Mussolini l'alleato*, pp. 1314ff, and Deakin, *The Brutal Friendship*, p. 395. After the Italian surrender, the Germans examined the Italian archives to ascertain whether Mussolini had had contacts with the Auglo-Americans, but they did not find any. See Weinberg, *A World at Arms*, p. 745 and n. 50.

67. On July 22, 1943, Foreign Ministry Director General Luca Pietromarchi wrote in his diary that Bastianini thought five conditions were necessary for breaking away from Germany: "1) that the Germans allow us to make a separate peace; 2) that the Duce agree to step down; 3) that a moderate government be formed to maintain power; 4) that the Allies

be disposed to deal with that government; and 5) that they offer acceptable conditions." Pietromarchi is cited by De Felice, *Mussolini l'alleato*,
p. 1338.

68. Cf. Dino Grandi's memoirs, *Il mio paese* (Bologna, 1985), and *25 luglio*.
In a long memorandum on these events that led to the coup of July 25,
sent in 1944 to U.S. Secretary of War Henry Stimson, Grandi portrayed
his role as one of opposition to Mussolini's pro-German stance. He
recalled that he had tried to bring Italy out of the war once before, in
May 1941, after the campaign in Greece, and then in the fall of 1942,
at the time of the Allied landing in North Africa. The text of Grandi's
letter to Stimson, dated March 1, 1944, and Stimson's letters of transmission are in 865.00/10–2344, RG 59, NA.

69. Letter of Dino Grandi to Secretary of War Henry L. Stimson, March 1,
1944, 865. 00/10–2344, RG 59, NA, p. 5.

70. On initiatives by the Action Party, see Giovanni De Luna, *Storia del
partito d'azione* (Milan, 1982), pp. 43–44.

71. See the statements of Maxim Litvinov, Soviet ambassador in
Washington, to Sumner Welles, November 6, 1942, in FRUS, 1942, vol.
3, *Europe*, p. 743.

72. FRUS, *The Conferences at Washington 1941–42, and Casablanca,
1943*, p. 749.

73. *The Diaries of Robert Bruce Lockhart*, vol. 1, p. 220, entry for January
9, 1943.

74. Eisenhower's uncertainty in the presence of two German divisions
aroused Churchill's anger. "'What Stalin would think of this,' Churchill
added, 'when he has 185 German divisions on his front, I cannot
imagine.'" See Martin Gilbert, *Winston S. Churchill*, vol. 7, *Road to
Victory, 1941–45* (London, 1986), p. 380.

75. Ibid., p. 439.

76. Among other ruses was the successful stratagem of allowing the
Germans to discover the plans for a landing in the Balkans on the corpse
of a man washed up on the shores of Spain. The project of announcing
a false armistice, however, was not complemented. On the plans for
landing on the island, see A. S. Cochran, Jr., *Spectre of Defeat: Anglo-
American Planning for the Invasion of Italy in 1943* (Ph.D. dissertation,
University of Kansas, copy at Ann Arbor, Mich.), 1985.

77. See Elena Aga-Rossi, "La politica degli alleati verso l'Italia nel 1943,"
Storia contemporanea 3, no. 4 (December 1972), pp. 847–95, later pub-
lished in *L'Italia nella sconfitta*, pp. 67–124; Harry L. Coles and Albert
K. Weinberg, *Civil Affairs: Soldiers Become Governors* (Washington,
D.C., 1964), pp. 170ff; Antonio Varsori, "'Senior' or 'Equal' Partner?"
Rivista di studi politici internazionali, 45 (April 1978), pp. 229–260.

78. Message from the Combined Chiefs of Staff to Eisenhower, May 24, 1943, *Bigot–Husky–Avalanche*, RG 84, NA.

79. See *The Italian Armistice*; F. H. Hinsley, *Intelligence in the Second World War: Its Influence on Strategy and Operations*, vol. 3, Pt. 1 (London, 1984), p. 102.

80. See Churchill to Roosevelt, July 16, 1943, and Roosevelt to Churchill, July 22, 1943, in *Churchill and Roosevelt*, vol. 2, pp. 329 and 341.

81. *The Italian Armistice*, p. 37, in Aga-Rossi, *L'inganno*, pp. 37, 121.

82. Ibid.

83. The exchange of messages is in FO 954/13, PRO London.

84. FRUS, *The Conference at Quebec, 1943* (Washington, D.C., 1970), p. 958.

85. On Ambrosio's position and that of the Supreme Command in the months before July 25, see the clear analyses by De Felice, *Mussolini l'alleato*, pp. 1117ff., and Deakin, *The Brutal Friendship*, pp. 166–69.

86. The text is in Comando Supremo, operational memoranda of General Castellano, *Collection of Italian Military Records*, L.T. 1154 a, NA, and is cited in De Felice, *Mussolini l'alleato*, p. 1133.

87. Mussolini argued that the Italians would have stopped the Allies "at the shoreline" (*bagnasciuga*), referring to the battle.

88. Ibid., p. 1134.

89. Ibid.

90. On the inglorious surrender of Pantelleria, see Alberto Santoni, *Le operazioni in Sicilia e in Calabria* (Rome, 1983), pp. 111ff. In the postwar period, it was often written that Pantelleria had surrendered for lack of water. According to Santoni there was no water problem; this was merely the justification Mussolini ordered Admiral Gino Pavesi, commander of the base at Pantelleria, to use to explain the surrender. In any case, the order arrived after Pavesi had already surrendered.

91. On Fascist propaganda in Sicily, see *Sicily: Handbook in Politics and Intelligence Service, 1943*, WO220/403, PRO.

92. The document is cited by Renda, *Storia della Sicilia dal 1860 al 1970*.

93. This document, a report from the territorial legion of the carabinieri in Messina, Enna Company, was confiscated by the Americans and is found among the OSS papers: MEDTO Sicily, entry 99, folder 195a, box 39, RG 226, NA.

94. Cited in Santoni, *Le operazioni in Sicilia e in Calabria*, pp. 229–30.

95. Ibid., pp. 243ff. The Fascist press and some postwar publications lauded the "heroic" resistance at Augusta.

96. Ibid., p. 250; Paolo Maltese, *Lo sbarco in Sicilia* (Milan, 1981), pp. 216–17.

97. Directive, *Mantenimento della disciplina e dell'ordine*, 1943, AUSSME, 1 RR, fasc. 7. "Milamart" refers to maritime artillery militia, a Fascist corps.

98. These data are given in Santoni, *Le operazioni in Sicilia e in Calabria*, p. 357.

99. See AUSSME, *Diario storico*, cart. 2228, Comando VI armata, and enclosures, July–August 1943, and especially July 23–30, 1943.

100. A summary of the thefts and acts of vandalism committed by the Germans is given in ibid., cart. 2135, Sicily.

101. Leonardo Sciascia, "L'eccidio di Castiglione," *La noia e l'offesa* (Palermo, 1976), pp. 145–46.

Chapter Two

1. On Dino Grandi's position, see P. Nello, *Un fedele disubbidiente. Dino Grandi da Palazzo Chigi al 25 luglio* (Bologna, 1993), pp. 408ff; Dino Grandi, *25 luglio quarant'anni dopo*, Renzo De Felice (ed.) (Bologna, 1983). On the fall of Mussolini, Renzo De Felice, *Mussolini l'alleato. L'Italia in guerra, 1940–1943*, vol. 2 (Turin, 1990), is essential.

2. The proposal was advanced by the king in a September 13 conversation with General Mason-MacFarlane, head of the Allied military mission to the Italian government, and was repeated by Badoglio in the king's name at Malta, where he had gone to sign the long armistice. See Mason-MacFarlane to Eisenhower, September 28, 1943, *Capitulation of Italy*, Eisenhower Library, Abilene, Kans., and Garland and Smyth, *Sicily and the Surrender of Italy*, pp. 548–49; Toscano, *Dal 25 luglio all'8 settembre*, pp. 222ff.

3. See Grandi's memorandum to Stimson, 865.00/10-2344, RG 59, Department of State Records, National Archives, Washington, D.C.

4. Puntoni, *Parla Vittorio Emanuele III*, p. 148.

5. Diary of General Ambrosio, in *Collection of Military Records*, I.T. 1223–26, NA, entries for July 27 and 31.

6. On the popular manifestations and the measures against them, see *L'Italia dei quarantacinque giorni* (Milan, 1969), pp. 6ff. The text of Roatta's circular is published in that book on p. 11, n. 49.

7. Actually, the Communist Party during the forty-five days was pursuing an intense propaganda campaign aimed at persuading soldiers to unite with the population in demanding an immediate peace. They distributed pamphlets with an appeal not to "fire on the people" and to unite with those demonstrating against the war and preparing to drive the Germans out (ibid., p. 334). Several anti-Fascist propaganda pamphlets are reprinted in the volume.

8. Directive by War Minister Sorice, August 1, 1943, *Commento alla truppa sulla situazione attuale*. See also *Azione morale sulle truppe nell'attuale situazione*, July 30, 1943, both addressed to all corps commanders and national defense commanders, and transmitted by these commanders to commanders of various sectors in the following days. See the texts of these directives in AUSSME, H5, RR1, fasc. 6, to which should be added that of Roatta of July 27, 1943, *Mantenimento della disciplina e dell'ordine*. See Chapter One, note 95, and the text related to it.

9. After the ministerial reshuffle suddenly decided by Mussolini in February 1943, Ribbentrop hastened to Rome, fearing indications that Mussolini was preparing for a separate peace, especially in view of Ciano's appointment as ambassador to the Vatican. Concerning this episode see De Felice, *Mussolini l'alleato*, p. 1050.

10. *War Diary of the Wehrmacht*, vol. 3, p. 382, cited in Schreiber, *I militari italiani internati*, p. 42.

11. On German plans for Italy before July 25, see Schreiber, *I militari italiani internati*, pp. 42–43; idem, "La linea gotica nella strategia tedesca. Obiettivi politici e compiti militari," in *Linea Gotica, 1944. Eserciti, popolazioni, partigiani* (Milan, 1993), pp. 25ff. Ralph S. Mavrogordato, "Hitler's Decision on the Defense of Italy (1943–1944)," in *Command Decisions* (New York, 1960).

12. Mavrogordato, "Hitler's Decisions on the Defense of Italy," p. 56.

13. See *Goebbels Tagebücher aus der Jahren 1942–1943* (Zurich, 1948), pp. 373ff. According to Hitler, a special unit was to enter Rome "to take over the whole mob, to rout out all that scum." See also *Hitlers Lagebesprechungen* (Stuttgart, 1962), p. 316. For Hitler's reactions and other evidence of his plans for a coup against Badoglio's government, see Schreiber, *I militari italiani internati*, pp. 55ff.

14. Goebbels's diary, entry for July 26, 1943, cited in Jens Petersen, "La Germania e il crollo del fascismo italiano nell'estate del 1943," in *La cobelligeranza italiana nella lotta di liberazione dell'Europa* (Rome, 1986), p. 317.

15. Ibid.

16. For the text, see *Hitler's War Directives, 1939–1945*, H. R. Trevor-Roper (ed.) (London, 1964). As far back as the beginning of July, German Armed Forces High Command had imposed on General Ambrosio the subordination of the Eleventh Italian Army to the orders of the German High Commander in the southeast (see Schreiber, *I militari italiani internati*, p. 67).

17. Mario Roatta, "Memoria sulla priorità dell'aggressione germanica," in AUSSME, *Diario storico*, II g.m., cart. 3000/a, doc. 42.

18. On the conduct of German forces after Mussolini's forced resignation, see J. Schröder, *Italiens Kriegsaustritt 1943. Die Deutschen Gegenmassnahmen in Italienischen Raum: Fall "Alarich" und "Achse"* (Göttingen–Zurich–Frankfurt/M., 1969), pp. 170ff.; idem, "La caduta di Mussolini e le contromisure tedesche nell'Italia centrale fino alla formazione del repubblica sociale italiana," in *L'Italia fra tedeschi e alleati* (Bologna, 1973), pp. 137–69; *Le operazioni delle unità italiane nel settembre–ottobre 1943*, pp. 24ff; and the note by the minister's chief of staff to Foreign Minister Raffaele Guariglia, July 31, 1943, in *DDI/9*, X, p. 745.

19. Roatta, "Memoria sulla priorità dell'aggressione germanica."

20. Palermo, *Memorie di un comunista napoletano*, p. 295.

21. See the minutes of the conversation between Italian Foreign Minister Guariglia and German Foreign Minister von Ribbentrop, August 6, 1943, in *DDI/9*, X, p. 774.

22. Ibid., p. 777.

23. Those supporting the view of a German betrayal include E. Kuby, *Verrat auf deutsch* (Hamburg, 1982), and more recently Schreiber, *I militari italiani internati*.

24. According to the testimony of Lieutenant Colonel Dogliani, head of the liaison unit between the Italian Supreme Command and General Kesselring, the latter refused to send an officer to Bolzano with Dogliani, who was to make sure that no incidents took place after the entry of the German divisions at the Brenner Pass, stating, "I do not know those people coming into Italy from the Brenner Pass, France or Tarvisio." Report on the events of September 8, 1943, in Marshal Kesselring's headquarters, OBS in Frascati, February 20, 1948, in AUSSME, *Diario storico*, cart. 3000/III/1.

25. In his memoirs, Kesselring writes that he viewed the "duplicity" of the Italians and Hitler as "intolerable" and that to the end he believed that, on the basis of collaboration with the Italian commands, Italy would go on with the war on the German side. See Albert Kesselring, *Kesselring: A Soldier's Record* (Westport, Conn., 1970), p. 212.

26. See the reports on German movements after July 25 and on the inaction of the military intelligence services in the memorandum "Secret Italo-German Collaboration after 25 July 1943," in FO 371/43874, PRO. See also the unpublished diary of Ambrosio, entry for July 30, 1943. On the ties between the militia and the Germans, see Attilio Tamaro, *Due anni di storia, 1943–45*, 2 vols. (Rome, 1948), vol. 1, p. 120.

27. See the interview with Ambrosio in D. Detwiler, C. B. Burdick and J. Rohwer (eds.), *World War II German Military Studies*, vol. 14

(New York, 1979), p. 18. See also the cited unpublished diary of Ambrosio.

28. Amé and Canaris met in Venice on August 2 and held a frank conversation on the Italian situation in which Canaris advised Amè to oppose the entry of additional German divisions into Italy. The meeting was requested by Marshal Keitel so that Canaris could be informed of Italy's real intentions. See Cesare Amè, *Guerra segreta in Italia, 1940–1943* (Rome, 1954), pp. 180–81; A. Brissard, *Canaris: The Biography of Admiral Canaris* (New York, 1974), pp. 315–16. See also John H. Waller, *The Unseen War in Europe: Espionage and Conspiracy in the Second World War* (New York, 1996), pp. 314–16.

29. Carboni had been appointed commander of the motorized corps for the defense of Rome on Roatta's proposal at the end of July, and according to Ambrosio, he was chosen to head the SIM because "he had anti-Fascist sentiments" (interview with Ambrosio in *World War II German Military Studies*, p. 18). According to Amè, the change was decided upon because of an intervention by Badoglio, with whom Carboni had very close contact. Minister of War Antonio Sorice told the commission chaired by Mario Palermo that Carboni reported to Badoglio as often as twice a day. See Puntoni, *Parla Vittorio Emanuele III*, p. 157, and Sorice's statement in Palermo, *Storia di un armistizio*, pp. 29ff.

30. AUSSME, *Diario storico*, cart. 2999, "Memoria sulla difesa di Roma," p. 8.

31. Ibid.

32. The memoirs of Roatta and Rossi, the books of Torsiello, Musco and Stefani, as well as the "Memoria sulla priorità dell'aggressione germanica" of Roatta, all summarize the content. In the archives of the Army Historical Office are excerpts of Memoria 44 based on the memories of officers in the various commands. The reference to the Communists is found in a document written later concerning the directives received by the Ninth Army Corps (AUSSME, H5, 1 RR, fasc. 9).

33. Roatta, "Memoria sulla priorità dell'aggresione germanica."

34. Roatta's testimony (see the record of his questioning by the Palermo Commission on December 22, 1944, in Palermo, *Storia di un armistizio*, p. 436) is in contrast to that of his close associates, Generals Zanussi and Rossi. They maintained that he was probably kept in the dark until mid-August about the decision to send emissaries for discussions of an armistice with the Allies. Zanussi wrote that Roatta informed him of Castellano's departure on August 16, but that he could not say whether Roatta was aware of the previous emissaries when he went to Bologna to negotiate with the Germans (Zanussi, *Guerra e catastrofe*, p. 75).

General Rossi of the Army General Staff, who accompanied Roatta to Bologna, wrote in his memoirs that on August 15 Roatta did not know that General Castellano "had already left Rome." Rossi, *Come arrivammo*, p. 102.

35. Palermo, *Storia di un armistizio*, pp. 436–37. Many historians, on the other hand, argue that Roatta asked the Germans to continue to defend the entire peninsula, since he was not aware of the negotiations with the Allies. See Stefani, *8 settembre 1943*, pp. 36 and 38.

36. See the Italian and German recommendations on the deployment of the two armies in Italy in Rossi, *Come arrivammo*, pp. 102–3. Ambrosio justified the move by arguing that the Italians controlled the landing sites in Sardinia and that a landing in force by the Anglo-Americans would in any case lead the Germans to withdraw. See the interrogation of Ambrosio by the Commission of Inquiry on October 15, 1944, and *Difesa di Roma*, doc. 7. More openly, Rossi wrote that, on August 15, "It was not yet certain that we would get an armistice" and therefore that "the movements studied by the Army General Staff responded exclusively to ideas for defending the peninsula against the Allies"; since "the two General Staffs thought a landing in Sardinia to be possible, it was obvious that the garrison of that Island should be reinforced with another armored division."

37. Statement of Ambrosio of November 15, 1944, to the Palermo Commission in AUSSME, *Diario storico*, cart. 3003. In another report, cited by Castellano, the original of which has not been found, Ambrosio justified his inaction by arguing that the "race to the ports" was so obvious that it could logically be applied even without specific orders on the initiative of the commander of the Army Group. Castellano, *La guerra continua*, pp. 149–50.

38. See Zangrandi, *1943. 25 luglio–8 settembre*, p. 469.

39. See Rossi, *Come arrivammo all'armistizio*, pp. 211–12.

40. For the British prisoners, the promemoria specified: "Prevent them from falling into German hands. Since it is not possible to defend all the camps effectively, the *white* prisoners may be set free, but in any case keep the *colored* ones." Other directives in the text made it clear that an armistice was possible; these included one to fire antiaircraft weapons at German aircraft but not at Anglo-American ones. The texts of the two promemorias are published in Aga-Rossi, *L'inganno*, pp. 339ff.

41. Ibid., p. 347.

42. The term "anti-Fascist" took on different meanings according to the persons who used it. As already noted, when the king asked the Allies to bring Grandi from Portugal to assume the post of foreign minister,

he presented him as a "symbol of the anti-Fascist movement." Garland and Smyth, *Sicily and the Surrender*, pp. 548–49.

43. *Lessons to Be Learned Regarding Unconditional Surrender as Applied to Italy*, memorandum of Major C. A. Harrison, Italian Region, to Mr. Duncan Wilson, German Region, January 1944, FO 898/410, PRO.

44. "An Armistice Quiz," note by the Resident Minister at Allied Force Headquarters, North Africa, August 10, 1943, in FO 371/37264, PRO, in Aga-Rossi, *L'Inganno*, pp. 269ff.

45. *New York Times*, May 17, 1943, p. 3.

46. See the statement of Churchill and Roosevelt in *The Italian Armistice*, pp. 38–39, in Aga-Rossi *L'Inganno*, pp. 121–22; for Eisenhower's message, see note 81 below.

47. Letter of Churchill to Roosevelt, July 26, 1943, in Churchill, *The Second World War*, vol. 5, *Closing the Ring*, pp. 56–58, and now in *Churchill and Roosevelt*, vol. 2, pp. 348–49.

48. Roosevelt to Churchill, July 30, 1943, in *Churchill and Roosevelt*, vol. 2, p. 366.

49. Ibid.

50. Memorandum entitled "Consiglio Corona," no date, E125, RG, NA.

51. Comment by Cavendish Bentinck on a memorandum of August 17, 1943, by P. Dixon (*Tactics of the Badoglio Government*), both in FO371.37265, PRO, London.

52. A copy of the OWI directives on Italy in this period, from which the following quotations are also taken, is located in the papers of Gaetano Salvemini, OWI, Istituto per la resistenza in Toscana, Florence.

53. On this episode, see John P. Diggins, *Mussolini and Fascism: The View from America* (Princeton, N.J., 1972), pp. 367–68.

54. *New York Times*, July 27, 1943, p. 16; *Washington Post*, July 26, 1943, p. 6.

55. Macmillan, *War Diaries*, p. 164.

56. *The Papers of Dwight D. Eisenhower*, vol. 2, p. 1288.

57. In sending the proposed armistice text to the Combined Chiefs of Staff (CCS) Eisenhower noted that it would not be possible to ask the Italians to attack the German forces, because the Italians "would deem it completely dishonorable to attempt to turn definitely against their former Allies." See Telegram from Commander in Chief to the CCS, July 27, 1943, 820. *Bigot–Husky–Avalanche, Post Caserta*, NA. Also cited in its entirety in *The Italian Armistice*, pp. 64–65, in Aga-Rossi, *L'Inganno*, pp. 147–48.

58. See "Surrender Terms for Italy and Draft Declaration and Proclamation," June 16, 1943, in CAB 88/12, PRO; Aga-Rossi *L'Inganno*, pp. 251–63. See the modifications approved by the American Joint Chiefs

of Staff and presented to Roosevelt on August 3, 1943, in FRUS, *The Conferences at Washington and Quebec*, pp. 538–47. For a comparison of the successive versions of the long armistice text, see the summary account in Aga-Rossi, *L'Inganno*, pp. 457ff.

59. Roosevelt to Churchill, August 2, 1943, *Churchill and Roosevelt*, vol. 2, p. 372.

60. On this occasion, Roosevelt recorded his opposition to the surrender terms for Italy presented by the British. "I did not like them because they attempted to foresee every possibility in one document. But, as so often happens when such an attempt is made, certain points were omitted and additional protocols with respect to naval and other questions had to be later presented." See the letter of Roosevelt to Churchill of February 29, 1944, transmitting the draft for the German surrender, in ibid., pp. 766–67.

61. Part of Churchill's letter to Eisenhower of July 29 is quoted, with Eisenhower's reply of the same day, in *The Papers of Dwight D. Eisenhower*, vol. 2, pp. 300–1. On the discussions following Eisenhower's proposal, see *The Italian Armistice*, pp. 66ff., in Aga-Rossi, *L'Inganno*, pp. 149ff.

62. Churchill, *The Second World War*, vol. 5, *Closing the Ring*, pp. 64–65.

63. "An Armistice Quiz."

64. On the hostility to Badoglio in court circles, see Puntoni, *Parla Vittorio Emanuele III*. On the position of the anti-Fascists, see Ivanoe Bonomi, *Diario di un anno* (Milan, 1947), passim. The quotation from De Gasperi is on p. 35.

65. Note of Consul General Berio at Tangier to Secretary General Prunas of the Foreign Ministry, in *DDI* 9/X, pp. 942ff.

66. Churchill to Roosevelt, August 5, 1943, in *Churchill and Roosevelt*, vol. 2, pp. 380–81.

67. See Guariglia, *Ricordi*, p. 647. This is a confirmation of Italy's deliberately ambiguous position.

68. See Castellano's report on his activities between August 12 and September 8, which he presented to General Ambrosio on December 15, 1943. It was published in Palermo, *Storia di un armistizio*, pp. 124–40, and is now in *DDI* 9/X, pp. 945–57.

69. The text of the telegram of Eden and Churchill can be found in a message of Eden to British ambassador Campbell in Lisbon, August 16, 1943, FO 371/37264.

70. On Guariglia's reaction, see his *Ricordi*, p. 669.

71. Telegram from Eden to Campbell, FO 37/37264; telegram from Eden to Churchill, August 16, 1943, Prem 3/249/3A, PRO.

72. The Declaration of Quebec is published in FRUS, *The Conferences at Washington and Quebec*, pp. 1060–62.

73. The British account of the meeting is in WO 106/3910 PRO. The Italian account was published in Castellano, *Come firmai l'armistizio*, pp. 210–18, and now in E. Aga-Rossi, *L'Inganno*, pp. 282–89.

74. On Alexander's position, see Murphy's message to Roosevelt of September 8, 1943, in FRUS, *The Conferences at Washington and Quebec*, pp. 1275–83.

75. It appears that Amè had a radio-telegraphic station installed in the Italian Embassy in Lisbon, with an operator and a hermetic code book prepared for the occasion, but no one thought to inform SIM of Castellano's mission. See C. De Risio, *Generali, servizi segreti e fascismo* (Milan, 1978), pp. 220–21.

76. See Carboni's memorandum, "Consiglio Corona." Carboni maintained that he became aware of the Castellano mission from a military intelligence (SIM) report in which the news was attributed to "ushers at Palazzo Vidoni [SIM headquarters] and some of General Castellano's lady friends" and that he was "very concerned" and took steps immediately. Roatta gives a different version of the decision to send General Zanussi, stating that communications broke off after Castellano's departure. Hearing nothing from Castellano, the Supreme Command asked Roatta to make another general available to be sent to Lisbon. Cf. Roatta, *Otto milioni*, p. 295. Montanari told the Commission of Inquiry that he had "good reason to believe" that Zanussi was sent because "General Roatta did not want to be excluded from the negotiations." See the "Minutes of the Interrogation of Consul Franco Montanari of December 12, 1944," in Palermo, *Storia di un armistizio*, p. 370.

77. Castellano professed surprise when General Smith gave him the text after the "short armistice" was signed on September 3, because no one had spoken to him about it (Castellano, *Come firmai l'armistizio*, p. 160). This failure to collaborate can, of course, be attributed to the absurd rivalry and mistrust between the two Italian officers, which is brought out by the reciprocal criticisms in their memoirs. However, it is also possible that Zanussi believed that the text Campbell gave him in Lisbon was the same one given to Castellano. In his testimony before the Palermo Commission on December 14, 1944, he stated that the British ambassador (Campbell) "informed me that Castellano had performed his mission and had left with a draft armistice of which I had a copy." Zanussi's interrogation in Palermo, *Storia di un armistizio*, pp. 140ff (the material quoted is on p. 141).

78. Zanussi, *Guerra e catastrofe*, pp. 92ff. Zanussi's letters to Carboni are in E125, RG 226, NA and in Aga-Rossi, *L'inganno*, pp. 290–91

and 294–95; the second letter dated August 29 is perhaps the message L. Woodward refers to in *British Foreign Policy*, vol. 2, pp. 493–94; he does not explain, however, that the decision not to allow Zanussi to return to Rome, thus changing the Foreign Office plans, was made so that Badoglio would not be told about the clauses in the long armistice. I have not found a copy of Zanussi's messages in AUSSME, but only in the files of the American intelligence services, probably sent by Carboni. Possibly they were destroyed along with other SIM papers.

79. See the account of these talks on August 31 in Murphy's message to Roosevelt of September 8, now in Aga-Rossi, *L'Inganno*, pp. 296–99 and 299–308.

80. In his memoirs Castellano maintains that the Allies were at the point of confiding the date of the landing to him, but Zanussi's arrival made them suspicious (*Come firmai l'armistizio*, p. 175), which is contradicted by Smith's letter of December 5, 1943, which Castellano cites as evidence.

81. See these points in Castellano, *Come firmai l'armistizio*, p. 144. The explanations of the landing south of Rome do not appear in the official account of the meeting, but in a supplementary document (ibid., p. 222).

82. Eisenhower's two messages to the CCS of September 1, 1943, were published in FRUS, *The Conferences at Washington and Quebec*, pp. 1257–61, and in *The Papers of Dwight D. Eisenhower*, vol. 2, pp. 1375–77. See also Stephen E. Ambrose, *Eisenhower: Soldier, General of the Army, President-Elect, 1890–1952*, 2d ed., vol. 1 (New York, 1985), p. 258. On the following day, Roosevelt and Churchill reiterated their concern in a telegram to Stalin in which they warned him that, given the urgency, it was possible that they might have the Italians sign the short armistice. The text of the telegram is published in FRUS, *1943, Europe*, pp. 360–61.

83. Castellano, *Come firmai l'armistizio*, p. 223.

84. Ibid., p. 224.

85. "Report on the Activities of General Castellano during the Negotiations Leading to the Conclusion of the Armistice," December 15, 1943, published in Palermo, *Storia di un armistizio*, pp. 120–40, and now in *DDI*, X, pp. 945–57.

86. AUSSME, *Diario storico, Castellano*, cart. 3000, in Agarossi *L'inganno*, pp. 397–98.

87. For the information held by the Anglo-American commands on the German plans, see Hinsley, *Intelligence*, p. 103. In Lisbon, Castellano said that thirteen German divisions were then in Italy, which surprised

the Anglo-Americans, who thought there were only four, aside from those in Sicily.

88. Nigel Nicolson, *Alex: The Life of Field Marshal Earl Alexander of Tunis* (New York, 1973), pp. 210–11.

89. See the series of reports on the Italian situation and the effects of Italy's collapse submitted to the Joint Chiefs of Staff, and in particular: "Collapse of Italy: Report by the Joint Intelligence Committee," July, 29 1943; "Occupation of Italy and Her Possessions, Report by the Joint War Plans Committee," August 7, 1943; "Effects of the Loss of Italy on the Axis Situation in Europe, Joint Intelligence Staff," August, 19 1943 – all in *CCS Italy, 1942–1945*, box 606, RG 218, NA. On the Allied belief that they would soon get to Rome, even after September, see Macmillan, *The Blast of War*, p. 407.

90. Alexander Papers, WO 214/36, PRO. Macmillan also informed Churchill of the decision not to inform the French in order to be sure of keeping the secret.

91. Ibid. Alexander even feared that a further transfer of the signature site to Algiers, where Allied Forces Headquarters were located, would give the Italians time for second thoughts, and he therefore telegraphed Eisenhower inviting him to fly to Cassibile, since "a move to Algiers might nullify what we have achieved." Telegram of Alexander to Eisenhower, September 2, 1943 (ibid.).

92. A list of the objectives assigned to the Italians is found in the Alexander Papers, "Tasks in Order of Priority" (ibid.), and is published in Aga-Rossi, *L'inganno*, pp. 398–99.

93. Alexander Papers, WO 214/36, PRO.

94. Ibid.

95. Memorandum of Admiral Raffaele de Courten, "Appunti da me tracciati a Brindisi il 10.9.43 sugli avvenimenti dal 3 al 9 settembre," in *Archivio storico della Marina* (Italian Navy Archive) (henceforth ASM), de Courten Memorandum, b. 1, fasc. 40.

96. See "Relazione sull'attività svolta dal generale Castellano durante le trattative," in *DDI/9*, X, pp. 954–55 (emphasis in original). The text of Castellano's report was annotated in the margins by Ambrosio, who made several critical observations, but there is no notation at this point. Castellano later explained that he had estimated the probable date of the landing from a confidential statement from Bedell Smith after the signing, according to which the landing would be carried out *within* two weeks (which would exclude one week). Castellano, *Come firmai l'armistizio*, pp. 172–73.

97. Ambrosio confided to de Courten on September 5 that "the time set for

the armistice is between the 10th and the 15th, more probably the 12th and 13th" ("Appunti da me tracciati"). In his written account, Roatta indicates September 3 as the day he received the news that the armistice had been signed and the other news, obviously not received until September 5, that the announcement would not be made before the 12th.

98. In the same passage in his memoirs, Roatta added that about fifteen Anglo-American divisions would be used in the landing, six for the defense of Rome and nine thereafter. This information was incorrect, because it contrasted with what Castellano had reported in the meeting of September 1. No one knows who fabricated this falsehood. See Roatta, *Otto milioni*, pp. 301–2.

99. See Roatta, "Memoria sulla difesa di Roma," p. 15.

100. Ibid., p. 16.

101. Ibid., p. 17 (emphasis in the original).

102. *Bedell Smith Collection: Capitulation of Italy*, Eisenhower Library, Abilene, Kans. Some of the messages are published in Italian translation in E. Aga-Rossi, *L'inganno*, pp. 310–11.

103. Roatta, *Otto milioni*, pp. 306–7.

104. The document can be found in AUSSME, *Diario storico, Castellano*, cart. 2235. It was published in Aga-Rossi, *L'Inganno*, pp. 337–39.

105. The text was published by Carboni in his memoirs (pp. 59–60) and in Palermo, *Storia di un armistizio*, pp. 349–51. See the "Reply of General Roatta of January 13, 1945, to the Note of September 6 Provided by General Carboni," in AUSSME, *Diario storico, Castellano*, cart. 2999. Ambrosio even denied that he had sent Castellano a written document, but this was rebutted by Castellano himself as well as by the fact that the document appeared in the list of papers destroyed on September 9. Castellano stated in his first interrogation that he had received the note of the 6th from Major Briatore, but he awkwardly withdrew this statement in a subsequent interrogation on February 27, in which he said, "I cannot exclude the possibility of having seen it … but as to the landing of six divisions in the Salerno–Naples area, I do not remember ever having read anything of the sort, and further, I believe I can exclude the possibility that it was known in Rome that the main landing was to take place in that area." Rossi made a similar statement on the preceding day, February 26, 1945. The two interrogations of Castellano and Rossi are published in Palermo, *Storia di un armistizio*, pp. 360–62 and 367, to which the reader is referred for a detailed account of the matter. Palermo, however, contends that the text Carboni presented was the same one that went to Castellano,

on the basis of the contradictory testimony given by Castellano and Rossi.

106. Transcript of the interrogation of Colonel Vincenzo Toschi, March 4, 1945, published in Palermo, *Storia di un armistizio*, pp. 364–66.

107. Ambrosio justified himself before the Commission of Inquiry by stating that he did not know about the arrival of the Allied officers. His false testimony was supported by Colonel De Francesco, according to whom Ambrosio had left for Turin without knowing of General Taylor's arrival ("Verbale dell'interrogatorio del ten. colonnello De Francesco," in AUSSME, *Diario storico, Castellano*, cart. 2999). Actually, Ambrosio knew of Taylor's mission and was the one who organized it. According to de Courten's testimony, Ambrosio asked him to send two motor torpedo boats to meet two British officials and transport them to Rome ("Appunti da me tracciati").

108. The Germans took over this fuel depot, which was defended by only a few men, an hour after the armistice was announced. See "Relazione del commandante Ventura, ufficiale di collegamento tra Supermarina e il Commando Supremo sugli avvenementi dal 25.VII al 10.IX," in ASM, de Courten memorandum, b. 1 fasc. 29.

109. Carboni, *L'armistizio e la difesa di Roma*, p. 29. Carboni was not aware of the pitiful impression he and Badoglio had made on Taylor and had "a firm impression that the brilliant American general, who for one day, in such a tragic moment, had been fully in his control. When he returned to the Allied General Headquarters, he would be an excellent and dedicated defender of the just Italian cause."

110. This is the text in English as found in the archives (Bedell Smith Papers) with the notation "Original message in Italian. This is a translation." See this and other messages exchanged between Rome and Allied Force Headquarters in Algiers during the night of September 7–8 in Aga-Rossi, *L'inganno*, pp. 311–17.

111. Badoglio, *La seconda guerra mondiale*, pp. 103–4.

112. Taylor also sent an account of the situation and a message with the word "innocuous," a code word for canceling Operation Giant 2. Taylor's messages are published in Italian translation in Aga-Rossi, *L'inganno*, pp. 313–14; see also Garland and Smyth, *Sicily and the Surrender*, pp. 488–89. In spite of irrefutable documentation, Italian historiography continues to support Badoglio's allegation that the Americans were the ones who wanted to cancel the operation. See the works cited in note 12 to the Introduction.

113. Among others favoring the operation were the military historian Samuel Eliot Morison, in *Sicily–Salerno–Anzio, January 1943–June 1944* (Boston, 1954), p. 241; and General Bedell Smith in a letter to

Castellano, in which he wrote: "Both I and the officers of the Operations Division are convinced that the plan could be executed successfully if a courageous, energetic and decisive officer were placed in command of the divisions deployed around Rome, who was confident of the possibility of success." The letter was published in Castellano, *La guerra continua*, p. 207.

114. There is a report on the McGregor Project in *Italy and Sicily*, MR, box 186, FDRL. According to this report, de Courten was aware of the project and "did not prevent communications, but also did not aid us before D Day." The expression "trump card" is in an OSS Berne report of April 13, 1943, OSS, MR, box 72, FDRL. See also the report from that source of April 26, 1943.

115. "Account of the Interrogation of Pietro Badoglio, Marshal of Italy, December 29, 1944," in Palermo, *Storia di un armistizio*, pp. 452–53. On Ambrosio's testimony, see note 37 above.

116. De Courten's memorandum, "Appunti da me tracciati."

117. This was the Dick memorandum, from the name of its author, Commodore Roger Dick, chief of staff to the commander in chief of Allied naval forces in the Mediterranean, Admiral Andrew Cunningham.

118. See de Courten's report on events in the Italian navy from September 5, 1943, dated February 12, 1944, in ASM, *de Courten – memoriale*, b. 1, fasc. 41, in Aga-Rossi, *L'inganno*, pp. 362–76.

119. See note 106 above.

Chapter Three

1. W. F. G. Jackson, *The Battle for Italy* (New York, 1967), p. 104.

2. This information was provided by Lieutenant Colonel Renato De Francesco during his testimony of December 14, 1944, before Mario Palermo's commission and was confirmed by Ambrosio. The two testimonies are published in Palermo, *Storia di un armistizio*, pp. 376 and 401. Sorice's statement can be found in a letter to Palermo of August 3, 1944. Ibid., p. 421.

3. Testimony of Aldo Visalberghi in Stefani, *8 settembre 1943*, pp. 287–88.

4. In the "Memorandum on the Defense of Rome," Roatta wrote: "The Government, the Supreme Command, and the Army General Staff logically believed that, even if the Allies had intended to move the schedule forward, this danger was no longer present. . . . It was beyond imagination that they would not wait until receiving a message of fundamental importance delivered by His Excellency [i.e., General] Rossi."

Roatta, "Memoria sulla difesa di Roma," p. 29. This whole text is underlined in the original.

5. "Note" dated September 8, 1943, unsigned, in AUSSME, *Diario storico, Castellano*, cart. 2235, now in Aga-Rossi, *L'inganno*, pp. 349–52.

6. Ibid.

7. In *Capitulation of Italy*, Bedell Smith Collection, in Aga-Rossi, *L'Inganno*, pp. 311–17.

8. Ibid. The text of Eisenhower's telegram, divided in transmission into four parts, is published in Garland and Smyth, *Sicily and the Surrender of Italy*, p. 507.

9. This comment on Badoglio is in de Courten, "Appunti da me tracciati."

10. Nearly all the participants gave their versions of the Crown Council meeting to the Commission of Inquiry. Luigi Marchesi provides an accurate account in his memoirs, *1939–1945, Dall'impreparazione alla resa incondizionata. Memorie di un ufficiale del Commando supremo* (Milan, 1993), pp. 75–82. See also Puntoni, *Parla Vittorio Emanuele III*, pp. 162–64. De Courten's version, in a note handwritten after the king and his party arrived in Brindisi, is as follows:

Summoned to his Majesty at 6 p.m. Shortly thereafter, a pale and exhausted Badoglio arrived with Ambrosio–Sorice–Sandalli, General Carboni, Maj. Marchesi and Guariglia. Ambrosio told me that Eisenhower has stated that he will announce the armistice at 6:30 P.M. and this nullifies the plan to move the troops in Croatia and Albania to the coast, as well as the American parachute operation on Rome.

Badoglio, Ambrosio and Guariglia came in first; then the others. They asked my views on X-Day. I replied that I knew nothing about it and that I had not been informed about the armistice terms. Then Ambrosio summed up the situation, saying that the armistice had been signed on the 3rd, with a verbal reservation to choose an appropriate date; but everything had been moved forward; protests had been made and Rossi had been sent to General Taylor in Palermo. It was hoped that Eisenhower could be convinced, but Reuters had already made public a story on the subject. Discussion: Guariglia said that he had always opposed this plan. A Stefani communiqué was being drawn up denying the Reuters story, when an officer came to inform us that Eisenhower had begun speaking. Tableau! I proposed that the king repudiate the government's actions, accept the resignations of everyone in it and appoint a new one. Some were in favor, others against. The king heard everyone out and then asked to be left alone. After ten minutes he summoned Badoglio and stated that he had decided to accept the armistice. Badoglio left for the broadcasting station, and while we went to the Supreme Command, where I saw the armistice clauses and the attached sheet for the first time. Disappointment: threat of scuttling the fleet. Ambrosio called my attention to what was written in the attached sheet.

See de Courten, "Appunti da me tracciati."

11. See "Verbale d'interrogatorio fatto al generale d'armata Vittorio Ambrosio in data 28 dicembre 1944," in Palermo, *Storia di un armistizio*, p. 403. See also Roatta, *Otto milioni*, pp. 333–34.

12. See "Verbale dell'interrogatorio fatto al maresciallo d'Italia Pietro Badoglio il 29 dicembre 1944," in Palermo, *Storia di un armistizio*, pp. 452–53.

13. The text of Badoglio's testimony is given in Stefani, *8 settembre 1943*, pp. 191ff. The statements quoted are on pp. 194 and 192, respectively.

14. Puntoni, *Parla Vittorio Emanuele III*, p. 167.

15. The order, signed by General De Stefanis for the chief of the General Staff, is in Palermo, *Storia di un armistizio*, p. 464.

16. See "Verbale dell interrogatorio fatto al maresciallo d'Italia Pietro Badoglio il 29 dicembre 1944," p. 453.

17. Carboni made this accusation not in his first volume of memoirs, but in a publication of 1952: *Più che il dovere. Storia di una battaglia italiana, 1937–1951* (Rome, 1952), pp. 246–47.

18. This testimony was given in a conversation between Dr. Franco Manaresi and Colonel Eugen Dollmam in Munich on February 4, 1984, in the presence of Monsignor Giulio Salmi. Dollmam stated that Berlin had not been informed of this decision, which could explain why neither he nor Kesselring mentioned it in his memoirs. The decision to let the king flee violated a direct order from Hitler. Dr. Manaresi left a report on Dollmam's statements at the Deputazione di Storia Patria in Bologna, but this has never been cited by historians. On the other hand, Dollmam's testimony by itself is not enough to establish that these events actually transpired. I thank Dr. Manaresi for allowing me to use this document, which was given to me by Renzo De Felice.

19. According to the historian Gerhard Schreiber, who has a military papers on Kesselring's operations in Italy, if there had been such an agreement, there should at least have been an order from Kesselring to the checkpoints, but no document of this kind has come to light. Further, Kesselring's silence on the matter at his trial in Venice in 1947,

where such an agreement would have been an important piece of evidence in his favor, is inexplicable. I thank Dr. Schreiber for supplying requested information in his letter of June 21, 1993. See also his analysis in *I militari italiani internati*, p. 112, n. 48. The theory that there was an agreement has also been rejected by Lussu, *La difesa di Roma*, pp. 295ff.

20. Giacomo Dogliani, "Relazione sugli avvenimenti dell'8 settembre 1943 dal tenente colonnello Giacomo Dogliani," p. 9.

21. According to Kesselring, on September 9 an Italian officer informed him that "they would offer no further resistance and were ready to talk." Kesselring, *A Soldier's Record*, p. 223.

22. The text of these orders can be found in the *New York Times*, September 9, 1943.

23. Giartosio, "Relazione sui giorni dell'armistizio."

24. Ibid.

25. De Courten's reluctance to order the hand-over of the fleet is evinced by his behavior, as already noted, in the days before the armistice and at the end of the Crown Council. Moreover, the copy of the armistice given him by Ambrosio on September 8 has the following handwritten note: "Remember that full execution is in the national interest." ASM, de Courten memorandum, b. 2, fasc. 47 (emphasis in the original).

26. See the list of radio messages from naval headquarters between September 8 and 10, following the announcement of the armistice in ASM, de Courten memorandum, b. 1, fasc. 41, in Elena Aga-Rossi, *L'inganno*, pp. 355–61. The tenor of these messages is confirmed by de Courten's report, of which they are an enclosure. In spite of these, even the studies that make use of this report, primarily the official history of the navy edited by Giovanni Bernardi, do not bring out this important fact, but reiterate that the fleet promptly carried out the order to put them out of their ports and proceed to Malta. Bernardi, *La Marina*, p. 65.

27. This attitude can be seen in the transcriptions of the radio messages sent from naval headquarters during those hours (ASM, De Courten memorandum, b. 1, fasc, 41, pp. 359–60; in Aga-Rossi, *L'inganno*, pp. 359–60). The episode is also described in Harry C. Butcher, *My Three Years with Eisenhower* (New York, 1946), p. 413.

28. Enrico Caviglia, *Diario, 1925–1945* (Rome, 1952).

29. "Promemoria per il generale Castellano," October 19, 1943, in AUSSME, *Diario storico, Castellano*, cart. 2238, fasc. "diplomazia 1."

30. See Mason-MacFarlane's letter to the War Office of October 6, 1943, in PREM 3/242/3, PRO.

31. Claudio Pavone, *Una guerra civile. Saggio storico sulla moralità nella resistanza* (Torino, 1991), p. 36.

32. Ibid., p. 14.

33. Testimony on the events of Trieste as recounted by Major Stefano Mascioli, in *l'Unità*, September 4, 1983, quoted by Pavone, *Una guerra civile*, p. 95.

34. M. Bernardo, *Il momento buono* (Rome, 1969), n. 25.

35. Beppe Fenoglio, *Primavera di bellezza* (Torino, 1991; 1st ed., 1959), pp. 109–110.

36. See the account by Andrea Pautasso Bert, who served at Aosta, north of Turin, in Stefani, *8 settembre 1943*, pp. 264–65. In this case, the order came from corps headquarters in Turin.

37. Schreiber, *I militari internati*, pp. 138–39.

38. For a careful analysis of events at Ascoli Piceno and Colle San Marco, see S. Bugiardini, *Memorie di una scelta. I fatti di Ascoli Piceno, settembre–ottobre 1943* (Ascoli Piceno, 1995). On resistance in the Abruzzi, see Costantino Felice, *Guerra, resistenza, dopoguerra in Abruzzo* (Milan, 1993), pp. 92ff.

39. Giovanni Messe to the minister of war and the chief of the Army General Staff, May 22, 1944, in AUSSME, L13, fasc. 27, sottofasc. "Arisio Mario, Pelligra Raffaele."

40. Ibid.

41. Torsiello, *Le operazioni delle unità italiane*, p. 204. The author fully justifies General Arisio's actions. Arisio was initially discharged; then the military tribunal held that Roatta was more to blame since he had authorized the transfer of headquarters and had failed to send any instructions.

42. These passages appear in a classified memorandum of the internal group headquarters of the Carabinieri Territorial Legion for Naples, dated October 4, 1943, immediately after the liberation of the city, in AUSSME, L13, fasc. 27, sottofasc. "Pentimalli." General Pentimalli was dismissed by the Royal Decree of January 27, 1944. The decision may have been related to the request for information on his behavior by the president of the Allied Control Commission, which was answered on February 2, 1944, by General Messe, AUSSME, L13, fasc. 27, sottofasc. "Pentimalli." Generals Pentimalli and Del Tetto were arrested after the liberation of Rome.

43. For example, the stronghold at Mondragone, near Naples, was held to the end, even though the area was bombarded by the Germans, and Colonel Michele Ferraillo died in hand-to-hand combat to avoid surrender. He was posthumously awarded the gold medal. See Torsiello, *Le operazioni della unità italiani*, p. 218.

44. Ercole Ronco, "Manifestazioni individuali e collettive di militari a seguito dell'armistizio," division commander's report, in AUSSME, *Diario storico, Divisione Nembo*, 184 Rgt. art.

45. Ibid.

46. Report on events in Sardinia dated June 4, 1944, signed by de Courten, in AUSSME, L13, racc. 33.

47. On the conduct of Italian troops in Sardinia, see the folder on General Basso in AUSSME, L13, and the report by Colonel Attilio Bruno in AUSSME, *Diario storico*, b. 2123, Reports on September 8, 1943, Armed Forces Headquarters in Sardinia.

48. On the episode at Maddalena see "Avvenimenti bellici ne La Maddalena dall'8 al 17/9/43," in AUSSME, *Diario storico*, b. 2123/2/2; Marina Addis Saba, "L'armistizio in Sardegna," in *8 settembre 1943. L'armistizio italiano 40 anni dopo*, p. 354.

49. The German commander, General Frido Senger und Etterlin, distinguished himself by his brilliant evacuation of the troops from the island, as well as for refusing to execute Hitler's orders to shoot as *francstireurs* the Italian officers captured after September 10, because "the officers had obeyed their legitimate government." F. Senger und Etterlin, *Combattere senza paura e senza speranze* (Italian trans.; Milan, 1968), p. 276. See also Gerhard Schreiber, "Lo sgombero delle truppe tedesche dalla Corsica," in *Le operazioni delle unità italiane in Corsica nel settembre–ottobre 1943*, Proceedings of the International Meeting Organized by the National Association of Combatants and Veterans (n.p., 1987), p. 133.

50. Filippo Frassati, "L'azione del comando supremo e dello SMRE tra il 25 luglio e l'8 settembre 1943," in *Le operazioni delle unità italiane in Corsica*, p. 107, n. 107.

51. Italo Calvino, "Angoscia in caserma," in *Ultimo viene il corvo* (Milan, 1988, 1st ed., 1949), pp. 106–7.

52. Summary of reports by military censorship officers for the month of September 1944, in E. Aga-Rossi, *L'Italia nella sconfitta*, p. 394.

53. Message from General Mario Arisio, commanding the Seventh Army, to the Supreme Command, September 17, 1943, AUSSME, *Diario storico*, b. 2004, allegati.

54. Bellomo was the only Italian general tried and condemned to death by a British tribunal for having fired in 1941 on a war prisoner trying to escape. The sentence was executed even though the trial had been conducted in a summary fashion. See the recent reconstruction by Fiorella Bianco, *Il caso Bellomo* (Milan, 1995).

55. For an overview of the resistance by Italian armed forces abroad see Gabrio Lombardi, *L'8 settembre fuori d'Italia* (Milan, 1966), and

Alfonso Bartolini, *Storia della resistenza italiana all'estero* (Padua, 1965). Among more recent works reflecting a renewed interest in the topic, see Alfonso Bartolini, *Per la patria e la libertà! I soldati italiani nella resistenza all'estero dopo l'8 settembre* (Milan, 1986); Biagio Dradi Maraldi and Romano Pieri (eds.), *Lotta armata e resistenza delle Forze Armate all'estero* (Milan, 1990); Schreiber, *I militari internati*. On the events in Cephalonia and Corfù see Giorgio Rochat and Marcello Venturi (eds.), *La divisione Acqui a Cefalonia. Settembre 1943* (Milano, 1993). In 1989 the Italian Defense Ministry commissioned a series of new publications concerning the resistance by Italian armed forces outside Italy. Among these see Pasquale Iuso, *La resistenza dei militari italiani all'estero. Isole dell'Egeo* (Roma, 1994).

56. See the ciphered message of the Combined Chiefs of Staff to the Commander in chief of the Allied forces in the Middle East, July 17 1943, in SOE Papers, HS 6/777, PRO, London.

57. For the text of the directive see *New York Times*, September 9, 1943.

58. Ambrosio's statement is cited in Castellano, *La guerra continua*, pp. 149–50.

59. See the war diary of the German admiral in charge of the Aegean sector cited in Schreiber, "Cefalonia e Corfù settembre 1943. La documentazione tedesca," in Rochat and Venturi, *La divisione Acqui a Cefalonia*, p. 130.

60. Schreiber, *I militari italiani*, p. 206.

61. PREM 3/245/7, PRO, in Aga-Rossi, *L'inganno*, pp. 413–15. The memorandum can also be found in Churchill, *Closing the Ring* (Boston, 1951), vol. 5, pp. 136–37.

62. Ibid.

63. Ibid.

64. "Chiefs of Staff Committee to J.S.M.," September 11, 1943, in PREM 3/245/7, PRO.

65. Churchill to the Joint Chiefs of Staff, September 14, 1943, in PREM 3/245/7, PRO. Note that Churchill goes from the expression "fight . . . with us" in his September 7 letter to "fight . . . for us" in that of the 14th. Probably Churchill was trying with this adjustment to persuade the Chiefs of Staff Committee that military collaboration with Italy would be useful.

66. Gilbert, *Winston S. Churchill*, vol. 7, pp. 502–4. Gilbert limits himself to an account of events, while McNeill, in going over the same facts, stresses the differing American and British strategies that came out on that occasion. William McNeill, *America, Britain and Russia: Their Cooperation and Conflict, 1941–1946* (New York, 1953), p. 305.

67. Eisenhower's text can be found in *The Papers of Dwight D. Eisenhower*, pp. 1407–8. Badoglio's reply is in AUSSME, *Diario storico, Castellano*, scat. 2235, in E. Aga-Rossi, *L'Inganno*, pp. 421–22. At Eisenhower's urging, Churchill and Roosevelt sent a message on September 11 exhorting Badoglio to lead the Italians in the struggle against the German invaders. See the text in *Department of State Bulletin*, September 11, 1943; see also Garland and Smyth, *Sicily and the Surrender*, p. 535.
68. See Woodward, *British Foreign Policy*, pp. 499ff (a similar request was made to the State Department), and Toscano, *Dal 25 luglio*, pp. 73ff.
69. The text of the message is in FRUS, *1943, II, Europe*, pp. 367–70. On the importance of this document and on its repercussions in the Allied camp, see Toscano, *Dal 25 luglio*, pp. 81ff, and Aga-Rossi, *L'Italia nella sconfitta*, pp. 121ff.
70. Churchill to Roosevelt, September 21, 1943, in *Churchill and Roosevelt*, vol. 2, pp. 458–59.
71. See *The Italian Armistice*, pp. 147–48, in Aga-Rossi, *L'Inganno*, p. 222.
72. Roosevelt to Eisenhower, September 23, 1943, Map Room, Control Commission, box 32, FDRL. The message is also published in FRUS, *1943, II Europe*, pp. 373–74.
73. See *Churchill and Roosevelt*, vol. 2, pp. 462–63; *The Italian Armistice*, p. 150, in Aga-Rossi, *L'Inganno*, p. 224.
74. Ibid.
75. The text of the message is published in FRUS, *1943, II Europe*, pp. 377–78.
76. Churchill to Roosevelt, September 28, 1943, in *Churchill and Roosevelt*, vol. 2, p. 470.
77. The question of whether to make public the text of the long armistice was brought up again by the Foreign Office in May 1944, when it became known that Badoglio had informed the members of the new government only about the clauses of the "short" armistice. A debate ensued within the British government, in which Churchill also participated, on whether to keep the long armistice secret (in FO 317/43792). On Eisenhower's commitment and the arguments for and against the publication, see Macmillan's memorandum "The Italian Armistice: The Long and the Short of It," PREM 3/250/2, PRO, in Aga-Rossi, *L'inganno*, pp. 440–45. Every subsequent Italian government was obliged to promise acceptance of the armistice, which was given to all cabinet members. They were required to keep it secret.

78. Dick Crossman to Sir Robert Bruce Lockhart, Algiers, September 14, 1943, FO 898/171, XC/80808.

79. Combined Chiefs of Staff message of September 21, 1943, WO 193/751, PRO. This file concerns operations in Italy from September 1943 to May 1944. See Butcher, *My Three Years with Eisenhower*, p. 639.

80. See also the letter of Noel Mason-McFarlane to the British War Office, dated October 6, 1943, PREM 3/242/3 PRO. On the belief in Germany's sudden collapse, see Butcher, *My Three Years with Eisenhower*, p. 639.

81. For the importance ascribed by the Germans to control of the Balkans, see the interview of General Wilhelm von Keitel by the Soviet intelligence services of June 17, 1945, published in *Neva*, no. 5 (1990), pp. 193–203, ed. Victor Ioltukhovsky, where Keitel states that the most important reason not to withdraw from Italy was to avoid losing Yugoslavia, which would be "condemned" in case of a withdrawal to the Alps.

82. Martin Gilbert dwells at length on the importance Churchill ascribed to the possession of Rhodes in *Winston S. Churchill*, vol. 7, pp. 509ff. On Castellano's attempt to commit the Italian ships to this operation, see the documents in AUSSME, *Diario storico*, cart. 2238.

83. Churchill to Roosevelt, October 7, 1943, in *Churchill and Roosevelt*, vol. 2, pp. 498–99.

84. Roosevelt to Churchill, October 7, 1943, in *Churchill and Roosevelt*, vol. 2, p. 501. The original and Leahy's draft are in the Map Room, box 4, FDRL.

85. Stimson Diary, Yale University Library, vol. 44, at October 12, 1943, in S. D. Mings, *Strategies in Conflict: Britain and the Anglo-American Alliance, 1941–1943* (Doctoral dissertation, University of Texas at Austin, 1975), p. 376. The dissertation can be consulted at the Hoover Library, Stanford University, California.

86. These expressions are taken from a letter of Churchill to Roosevelt of October 26, 1943, in *Churchill and Roosevelt*, vol. 2, pp. 562–63. Roosevelt did not respond to Churchill's request.

Conclusion

1. Even some British and American authors share this interpretation. Examples are David Ellwood in his *Italy, 1943–1945* (Leicester, 1985), which is nevertheless a fundamental study of the topic, and James

Edward Miller in *The United States and Italy, 1940–1950* (Chapel Hill, N.C., 1986). For a criticism of works on the relations between the Resistance and the Allies, see Elena Aga-Rossi, "La politica anglo-americana verso la resistenza italiana," in *L'Italia nella seconda guerra mondiale e nella resistenza* (Milan, 1988), pp. 141ff.

2. Even Roatta maintains that when Ambrosio informed him of General Castellano's mission, he agreed and added that in his view it was not "sufficient to stop fighting the Anglo-Americans, but indispensable to take up the struggle at their side against the Reich" (*Otto milioni*, p. 295). This statement is refuted by our account of the facts.

3. Foreign Office Research Department, "A Summary of Reports Furnished by the Psychological Warfare Branch, Allied Force Headquarters, Mediterranean, Regarding the Political Events in Italy between 24th July and 8th September, 1943," dated January 20, 1945, FO/371/49759, PRO.

4. "Relazione sugli avvenimenti dell'8 settembre 1943 del tenente colonnello Giacomo Dogliani."

5. Pavone, *Una guerra civile*, p. 94.

6. Fenoglio, *Primavera di bellezza*, p. 111.

7. The presence of many soldiers from the former Royal Army in the first partisan bands is mentioned in one of the first documents of the Communist-inspired "Garibaldi brigades," which states: ". . . the partisan detachments arose as a spontaneous reaction of the people and the army against German occupation and Fascist betrayal. They often developed around a worker, intellectual, soldier, graduate or an energetic and decisive officer able to organize them and keep them going. . . . [T]hese detachments for the most part had no specific political configuration other than deep-rooted hatred for the Germans and the Fascists." This excerpt is from a document with a handwritten note, "September 1943," Archivio Istituto Gramsci (3-1-18), Rome, and has been published in *Le brigate Garibaldi nella resistenza*, 2 vols., ed. Giampiero Carocci and Gaetano Grassi (eds.) (Milan, 1979), vol. 1, pp. 101–2.

8. Though not standard, the following words of Leonardo Sciascia illustrate this schematization as they deny the "badogliani" any legitimacy: "[B]etween the Garibaldi formations and those of 'Giustizia e Libertà' there was even this difference that the first were fighting for a new world and the others for a form of loyalty and obedience to the king. In one sense, many young men in the army of the Italian Social Republic were closer to the spirit of the Resistance, in the illusion of a social revolution delayed for twenty years by collusion between Fascist hierarchs, 'traitors with the forces of capitalism, the monarchy and the Vatican,'

than certain combatants in the partisan formations" (*La noia e l'offesa*, p. 163).

9. This is shown by the incisive analysis of Gian Enrico Rusconi, *Se cessiamo di essere una nazione* (Bologna, 1993). The author gives ample space to the patriotic aspect of the Resistance.

Index

Index

proclaimation, 103–15; as
prisoners of German forces,
104, 111, 114–15
Italian Supreme Command:
assignments according to
armistice agreement, 81–2, 84;
assumptions and actions related
to Anglo-American landings,
61–2, 82–9; continued
collaboration with Germans,
61–2, 108–9; decision not to
defend Rome, 96, 98–9; flight
from Rome, 1; informed of
Allied airborne troops to be
sent, 79; missions assigned for
Anglo-American landing in
Italy, 81–5; mistrust and
divisions among, 72–3;
negotiations with Allies, 74–5;
order about responses to
Germans (September 9, 1943),
97; ordering collaboration with
Germans (1943), 62; orders not
to oppose Germans, 97, 102–3;
orders to Italian troops in
Greece and the Aegean, 63;
post-Mussolini delay in
contacting Allies, 43–4; postwar
inquiry of, 3–4; predicted site of
Anglo-American landing in
Italy, 64
Italy: attempts to contact Allied
forces (1942), 33; British
prediction of collapse of, 37;
British strategy against
(1940–1943), 11–12; causes of
collapse, 37; defeats in Africa
and Russia (1942), 32–3;
negotiations between Anglo-
Americans and, 63–4; objectives

in negotiations with Allies,
73–5; reaction to Mussolini's
fall, 65; strategic importance to
Germany of, 54; uprisings
following Mussolini's
resignation, 53

Kerr, Clark, 38
Kesselring, Albert: Allied air raids
on headquarters of, 94;
continued occupation of Rome,
102; decision to take control of
Rome, 99; on Italy's request for
armistice, 132; loses Hitler's
confidence, 58; modification of
German withdrawal, 80; plan
for withdrawal from Rome,
98–9

La Malfa, Ugo, 134
landing in Italy, Allied: Badoglio's
strategy of deception related to,
82–3, 87–9; in Calabria and
Salerno, 41, 106; canceling of
Operation Giant 2 paratroop
drop, 88–9; errors in predicting
German response to, 80–1, 122;
expectations about, 102, 122;
Italian assumptions about,
91–4, 101–2; Italian defensive
measures against, 62, 129;
misinformation conveyed to
Italians about, 77–82, 126;
operational plan, 84; paratroop
landing, 84–5
landing on Sicily, Allied (July
1943), 39–40
Lanza d'Ajeta, Blasco, 73
Leahy, William D., 123
Lockhardt, Bruce, 20

Index

Loraine, Percy, 13
Lussu, Emilio, 15, 36

Macmillan, Harold: on idea and
 meaning of unconditional
 surrender, 64–5, 71–2; on
 Italian signing of armistice, 81;
 changes opinion on signing of
 long armistice, 120
Magli, Giovanni, 110–11
Malta meeting: Eisenhower at,
 119–21; signing of long
 armistice at, 121
Marchesi, Luigi, 84, 95
Marino, Ettore, 107–8
Mason-McFarlane, Noel, military
 mission to the Italian
 government and
 recommendation not to impose
 long terms, 119
Mazzini Society, 36
Mediterranean theater: Allied
 strategy in (1941), 13–20;
 British and American strategy
 disagreement, 37–42. See also
 Aegean Islands; Corsica; Ionian
 Islands; Pantelleria island;
 Santorino; Sardinia; Sicily
Messe, Giovanni, 4, 106–7
Military leaders, Italian: pro- and
 anti-German, 66–7
Molotov, Vyacheslav, 120–1
Murphy, Robert, 29
Mussolini, Benito: Allied
 interpretation of his fall from
 power, 65–6; "*bagnasciuga*"
 (shoreline) speech, 43; fall of
 (July 25, 1943), 37, 41, 50,
 65–6; leaning toward separate
 peace with Soviet Union,

34–5; pressured to exit the
 war, 35

Naples: abandoned to the
 Germans, 3, 107–8; civilians in
 defense of, 108
naval operations, Italian: related to
 armistice terms and Allied
 landing, 89–90, 100–1
Normandy landing (Overlord): no
 diversion from, 123;
 preparation for, 38; Soviet
 support for, 124
Northern League, 137

Orlando, Vittorio, 50
Overlord, priority of, 123

Palermo, Mario, 3, 86
Palermo Commission of Inquiry,
 3–4, 61, 86–7, 96
Pantelleria island: fell of, 43
partisan bands: Greece, 115;
 Italian, 106, 135–6
Pavone, Claudio, 103, 135, 137
Pelligra, Raffaele, 106
Pentimalli, Riccardo, 3, 107–8
prisoners, allied, 69, 106; helped
 by the population, 104
prisoners, Italians, taken by the
 allies, 69; taken by the Germans
 after the armistice, 2, 104–5,
 111, 114–15
propaganda, Allied: after
 announcement of armistice,
 100; British strategy against
 Axis (1940–1941), 10–12; idea
 of honorable capitulation, 64–5;
 promises to surrendering
 Sicilian soldiers, 46; related to

Index

acceptance of, 131; mentioned in meetings and documents of the state department, May–November 1943, 21–3; position of U.S. government on, 20–3, 70; proclamation by Roosevelt of, 23–5; rigid application of, 113. *See also* armistice, Italian/Allied.

United Nations. *See* Allies

United States: disagreement with British over strategy in Mediterranean, 37–42; favoring separate peace with Italy, 14–15, 20; fear of separate Soviet peace with Hitler, 38; Joint Chiefs opposition to Italian campaign, 127; Joint Chiefs reject text of long armistice, 31; military strategy to defeat Axis, 37–42; policy of Italy's unconditional surrender, 14–15, 20–1, 29; position on de facto recognition of Italian government, 70; position on Italian monarchy, 27–8

Vichy regime, France, 135

Victor Emmanuel III (king of Italy): Allied perception of, 126; Allied position on retention of, 69–70; assumptions about

Allied landings in Italy, 102; dismissal of Mussolini, 50–1, 133; fear of contacting Allies, 52; flight from Rome (September 9, 1943), 1, 97–8, 101–2, 128–9, 133; inability to lead Italy, 129, 131, 133; keeping options open, 92, 95, 102; overtures to Allied governments, 34; position of not opposing Germany, 96–7; position on unonditional surrender, 72; Roosevelt's communications with, 14; U.S. propaganda against, 67–8; weaknesses and failures of, 59–60, 128–31

Visalberghi, Aldo, 92

War Cabinet, Britain: approves policy of unconditional surrender but opposes Italy's exclusion, 23; position on separate peace with Italy, 18–19

Welles, Sumner, 14

Wheeler-Bennett, John, 28

Wilson, Henry Maitland, 100, 113, 122

Zanussi, Giacomo: actions related to long armistice, 76–7; role in armistice negotiations, 77, 92